DORIS LESSING

DORIS LESSING

An Annotated Bibliography of Criticism

Compiled by
DEE SELIGMAN

GREENWOOD PRESS
Westport, Connecticut • London, England

Library of Congress Cataloging in Publication Data

Seligman, Dee, 1944-
    Doris Lessing : an annotated bibliography of
criticism.

    Includes index.
    1. Lessing, Doris May, 1919-   --Bibliography
Z8503.8.S44   [PR6023.E833]   016.823'914   80-24540
ISBN 0-313-21270-8 (lib. bdg.)

Library of Congress Catalog Card Number: 80-24540
ISBN: 0-313-21270-8

First published in 1981

Greenwood Press
A division of Congressional Information Service, Inc.
88 Post Road West, Westport, Connecticut 06881

Printed in the United States of America

10 9 8 7 6 5 4 3 2 1

CONTENTS

PREFACE

Despite the growth in interest in the work of Doris Lessing during the seventies, no complete bibliography has been done since 1973 when Selma R. Burkom and Margaret Williams created a *Checklist of Primary and Secondary Sources* (Troy, New York: The Whitston Publishing Co.). Yet the Modern Language Association has had a seminar on her work since 1971, a Doris Lessing Society and *Doris Lessing Newsletter* (available from Paul Schlueter, Editor, 314 McCartney Street, Easton, Pennsylvania 18042) has been established, and dissertations are being written every year. The need for a current annotated bibliography seems clear. This bibliography attempts to be comprehensive through 1978.

I have tried to be as useful as possible to the Lessing reader so that appropriate material can be found easily and the rest can be ignored. To this end, the annotations are not merely descriptive but also evaluative. I have provided an easy method of surveying the development of criticism on Lessing by organizing the entries in chronological rather than alphabetical order in certain sections. All of the primary work is organized chronologically, as are all of the translations of her work. Within Section III, Works About Lessing, the following sections are organized chronologically: book-length criticism, general criticism, references to Lessing in other books, the list of Modern Language Association papers on Lessing, and dissertations. In other words, all of the sections which provide information on the secondary material which might be of interest for a chronological survey are so listed. All of the other material is listed alphabetically.

Unfortunately, two citations could not be identified properly, although I attempted to find this information right up until the time this bibliography was published. I received two pieces on Lessing from Mr. Derek Robinson of Great Britain, who had been provided with some material on Lessing by the BBC Radio's Information Department. Unfortunately, the BBC didn't respond to my inquiry, and neither piece is indexed according to my own research. Both pieces are worth seeking out, and perhaps some British reader might provide all of us with the necessary bibliographic information. Entry #78 is a biographical sketch by Lessing of Idries Shah and begins with a description of how Lessing became his student. Entry #103 is titled "Portrait of a New Nation" and is dated 3 January 1965. It concerns Lessing's visit to Zambia and appears to be out of a British newspaper Sunday supplement.

This bibliography could not have been done without the assistance of certain libraries and individuals. I am particularly grateful to the Wellesley College Library, and especially to Mrs. Linden and Mrs. Stockard, for their assistance. Boston University's inter-library loan and reference divisions were equally helpful. Many individuals offered their support, and lo, most unusual in these hard times, even some of their own research to me. They include: Ellen Cronan Rose, Malcolm Page, Sallie T. Hightower, Nancy Topping Bazin, Paul Schlueter, Claire Sprague, Roberta Rubenstein, and Martha Lifson. Members of the newly formed Doris Lessing Society were equally kind to me and helped me understand the importance of this project. Finally, I wish to thank Roz Cooper for her time spent with my children, Janet Dinarello for her patience in typing, and my children and husband, Adam, Justin, and Larry for their quiet suffering with late night typing.

Both Doris Lessing and her critics wish to be read. If this work helps others to find out more quickly what to read, it shall have served its purpose.

INTRODUCTION TO DORIS LESSING

I HER LIFE

Doris Lessing has provided a distinctly humanistic voice for our time. She has never been content with merely cataloguing the restrictions of sex, nationality, or social class, but rather has spoken eloquently of our daily existence in a language informed with sensitivity to the dissonant rhythms of our socio-political environment. Her work, which began in 1950 with the publication of her first novel, *The Grass is Singing*, has spanned many forms: novels, short stories, plays, poetry, essays, reportage, book reviews, and autobiographical narratives, to name but a few. Her topics reflect many of the concerns of our time: racism, feminism, Marxism, psychoanalysis, madness, extrasensory perception, and mysticism, but she has generally addressed herself to these concerns before they became part of the popular mind-set. She writes not only about the historical past, but also about the imagined future. Yet there is a unity within this variety which is seldom found in such a prolific career. Her perspective on her material has always been the "small personal voice" of the writer, that detached and sometimes ironic listener who is nonetheless passionately committed to the survival of the human species. She has never concentrated on promoting any one group at the expense of another but has always insisted that the survival of all is dependent on the existence of the integrated individual. Seriousness, discipline, solitariness, and unflinching honesty are the necessary ingredients for those who would actively seek this integration. They are also qualities which describe Lessing's style as a writer. She is considered one of the leading novelists of our time because she confronts with vision and intelligence our current situation.

One would find it difficult to predict that a writer of this stature would grow up in surroundings as isolated and primitive as those of Doris Lessing's youth. Born in Persia (Iran) in 1919, Doris was the first born child of Alfred Cook Tayler and Emily (Maud) McVeagh. Her father was a British bank official, and her mother was his former nurse following a World War I hospitalization. Doris had a younger brother, Harry, born two years later. The family moved to what was then Southern Rhodesia and is now Zimbabwe to take up farming in a small town, Banket, in an effort to colonize this southern African country.

The family was very poor, scratching out a living by raising maize and tobacco. They lived in a mud and pole house with Gloria flour bags for clothing and petrol boxes for furniture. Lessing's early years are reflected upon in her 1956 book *Going Home* and also in her novel *Martha Quest*. Her home life was in many ways distressing; her parents' marriage was not a happy one. Her father's lack of financial success directly contradicted his expectations when setting out to colonize this country in 1925. His leg had been amputated, and he was frequently medicated. He was a dreamer who became a cynic, and his disillusionment and subsequent frustration left their mark on his daughter. Oddly enough, a remark from her father serves as a preface to her 1979 novel *Shikasta*: "For my father, who used to sit, hour after hour, night after night, outside our house in Africa, watching the stars. 'Well,' he would say, 'if we blow ourselves up, there's plenty more where we came from!'"

Doris never really got along with her mother, perhaps because she was such an independent and solitary child. Her mother had been a nurse with much supervisory responsibility, and she never gave up her domineering attitude. Furthermore, she was unhappy living in Africa and longed to return to England where life would be normal, filled with dinner parties and musical evenings. Doris Lessing has said that both her mother and father were in "complicated emotional states," and she was under "terrible pressure as a child, which is true of every child, mind you, but I think it was slightly worse in my case."[1] She was not only emotionally isolated, but also physically isolated. She grew up as one of two white women on a farm composed of African laborers, surrounded by miles and miles of open veldt upon which she and her brother hunted small game for food.

She was sent to a Catholic high school in the capital city of Salisbury for her high school education, but she left it in 1933 when her eyes gave her trouble. She continued reading at home, but she had no formal education after age fourteen. She never attended a university and has little use for those whose university educations have failed to encourage independent thinking. She is often regarded by critics as having tremendous intellectual curiosity and a wide range of knowledge. Even when she was a young girl this capacity was recognized. Her brother has stated that she was given her first job at the telephone company in Salisbury on the basis of a list of the books she had read in the previous six months.[2]

In 1939 she married a civil servant named Frank Wisdom by whom she had two children, a boy, John, and a girl, Jean. The marriage ended in divorce in 1943, and the children remained with their father, who later remarried.

Doris taught herself typing and shorthand and worked first as a legal secretary and then later as a Hansard secretary (equivalent to a court stenographer) in the Rhodesian Parliament. During the war years she became actively involved in politics and worked with the only progressive party of that time, the Southern Rhodesian Labour Party. Although there was no real Communist party in Rhodesia at that time, she was also a participant in a small Marxist group, along with many immigrants and foreign servicemen stationed in Southern Rhodesia. This political group was primarily concerned with the oppression of the blacks in Rhodesia.

In 1945 she married Gottfried Lessing, a half-Jewish German immigrant who was a Communist and active in the Marxist group. She bore a child, Peter, in 1947, and he remained with his mother after the couple was divorced in 1949.

In that year the Lessings left Southern Rhodesia for England, where Doris and her son settled while Gottfried went directly on to East Germany. Doris Lessing brought with her the manuscript of her first novel, *The Grass is Singing*. It was published by Michael Joseph, the first English publisher approached by the author, and was a great success, being reprinted seven times within five months of its publication.[3]

She has remained in England since then, and her writing has continued almost without a break from that time. She has traveled to Russia, to continental Europe, and even in 1956 back to Rhodesia, but London has been her real home since 1949. Her visit to Rhodesia in 1956 resulted in an official ban on her travel to that country as a "prohibited immigrant" because of her Communist affiliations. She actually joined the Party in England but insists that she never really attended meetings.[4] She left it officially in 1956 after the Twentieth Party Congress and the revelation of Stalin's atrocities and the invasion of Hungary. However, her work has been clearly influenced by Marxism both in its content and in its use of a dialectical form.

Although access to Lessing for interviews has become more difficult as her literary stature has grown, she has always tried to reach large numbers of people in her writing. She has never considered herself an academic or esoteric writer, and her literary career attests to her desire to be heard. In the late fifties she participated in mass demonstrations, speaking at a Campaign for Nuclear Disarmament (C.N.D.) meeting, joining in demonstrations against rocket bases, and speaking at the first Aldermaston March (April 1958).[5] She also served until late 1961 on the editorial board of *The New Reasoner*, an independent Marxist publication which later evolved into the *New Left Review*.[6] She must have been working on *The Golden Notebook* during this time, since it was published in 1962. During the early sixties she also worked in the theater, helping to establish Centre 42, a type of populist arts program, and writing her own play, *Play With a Tiger*, which was published in 1962.[7] She had had three plays of her own performed by 1960 and filled in as a theater reviewer for *The Observer* in 1958.[8] She chose two mass distributed paperback houses—Ballantine Books and Bantam Books—as American publishers for many of her works. She even wrote a "Letter to the Editor" in 1972 requesting that more paperbacks be reviewed since publishing in paper was clearly the direction the industry ought to be headed if good reading material were to be available to all.[9]

In the late sixties her thinking came under the influence of Idries Shah, a teacher of that mystical form of Islam known as Sufism. The emphasis of Sufism is against preconceived or inherited ideas. It is an optimistic philosophy which presents human beings as capable of conscious evolution of their higher faculties in order to exist humanely in societies as structured and programmed as ours. The human community is perceived as an integral unit, and individuals can become part of the evolution of this unit if they are deliberate in their efforts. No one is considered exceptional to a Sufi; the accomplished are simply those who have tapped the hidden potentialities within us all. Extrasensory perception is one of these potentialities within the realm of all people, but we must free ourselves of rationalistic notions of the human mind. Sufism impressed Lessing with its systematic, albeit non-rational, observation of the workings of the mind. Shah's teaching is quite apparent in Lessing's work since *The Four-Gated City* (1969).

II HER NOVELS

One is ultimately attracted to Lessing's work not because she represents Sufism or Marxism or feminism or any of the other "isms" which get grafted onto her name, but because she is an intellectual writer with wide political experience who draws from her experience with sensitivity and perspective. Her works matter in our day to day lives; they speak to our concerns as women, as men, as Westerners, as progeny of European colonialists, as racists, as oppressed races, as rationalists, as "crazies," and most importantly, as the potential victims of some dreaded holocaust. While each work provides a slightly different accent, all her works taken together compose a language with which we can verbalize what has happened in the West since the First World War.

The Grass is Singing (1950) is an intense, realistic portrait of a woman's breakdown as she confronts her own neuroses and those of the racist culture in which she was raised. Mary Turner, an unpopular and unsure girl, finally marries and comes to live on a farm with an unsuccessful husband. She is surrounded by black farm workers whom she despises and is served personally by a black houseboy named Moses. She is isolated and spiritually desiccated, as is the white society she embodies. She becomes more and more dependent on her relationship to Moses for her personal vitality, and yet her metaphysical sense of order is more and more disturbed by this dependency. She "breaks down" as her sense of reality becomes disoriented. This portrait of madness is more fully developed in later works by Lessing. Finally, Moses murders Mary. Her life and her death as depicted are the product of the social realities of a patriarchal, colonial system.

The Children of Violence (1952–1969) series examines that system in great depth. This series consists of five novels published over a seventeen year period; they were Lessing's only serial novels until 1979 when she began the publication of the *Canopus in Argos* series. The *Children of Violence* series traces the protagonist, Martha Quest, from her adolescence on a small farm in the mythical country of Zambesia ("a composite of various white-dominated parts of Africa," Lessing states) to her adulthood in London as personal secretary and parent surrogate in the home of a wealthy writer, Mark Coldridge. The series presents the relationship between the individual and the social institutions in which she or he voluntarily and involuntarily participates. As Lessing's protagonist pursues a deeper and deeper understanding of her self, Lessing provides extensive documentation for our time on the nature of marriage, left wing political activity, child rearing, racial strife, war, education, and patriarchal privileges, while simultaneously documenting our sense of frustration, fragmentation, and disintegration. Lessing's protagonist finally recognizes that her search through many social classes and through the continents of Africa and Europe actually should have been an internal search, a journey into the solitude of her own experience as it resonated with the collective experiences of all human beings. The effect of these five novels on the reader is powerful; their sweep over time and events recalls the great nineteenth century Russian novelists, whom Lessing much admires. Yet Lessing provides a more refined probing of the psychology of her own generation. It is this convergence of history, psychology, and prophecy which frames Lessing's unique vocabulary.

The Golden Notebook, published in 1962, marks a pivotal point in Lessing's career. It records the life of Anna Wulf from the war years of World War II until 1957. Its form is complex, consisting of four notebooks, a novel within a novel, and a final notebook, also entitled "The Golden Notebook." Anna's life is also complex, consisting of a close relationship with a woman friend, Molly, with Molly's son Tommy, with her own daughter, Janet, and with two lovers, first Michael, and then Saul Green. Anna is a novelist, suffering from a writer's block; before she can continue her novel she must face her own sense of fragmentation, of impotence in improving the social injustices of our time, of distrust of "reality" and language, and of frustration over her dependency on men. Lessing has stated that she wanted to write a book which created "a new way of looking at life," which would "break certain forms of consciousness and go beyond them." In this long novel, Lessing concentrates on using the form of the novel itself to communicate, and what she communicates is the likelihood that the rational mind which catalogues, systematizes, and shuts out is inadequate to cope with the experiences of women in this century.

The other three novels covered by this bibiliography were all published during the first half of the seventies: *Briefing for a Descent into Hell* (1971), *The Summer Before the Dark* (1973), and *Memoirs of a Survivor* (1974). All three experiment with form to some degree, particularly in their use of material from the unconscious, from memory and dream, as counterweights to the rational mind. *Briefing* concerns a classics professor, Charles Watkins, who, because of amnesia, was put in a mental hospital. He is, in fact, one of those chosen by the "gods" to warn us of our future self-destruction. Watkins eventually agrees to shock therapy and loses the important memory of his role of messenger from the "gods." He returns therefore to the ordinary world, that is, to the confines of limited consciousness. Similarly, the protagonist of *The Summer Before the Dark* returns to function in "our" world, but she is utterly changed after a separation from her family and its lifestyle and her experience of a nervous breakdown. Kate Brown is not only an accessible and hence effective character, the middle-class white woman, but also her dream life, of a seal which must be released to the water, serves as an effective symbol of her psychic growth. Her interactions with a young woman, Maureen, who is on the verge of making some important decisions about her own life, provide a foil for the decisions which Kate must make about her life.

The Memoirs of a Survivor, like *The Summer Before the Dark*, uses experimentation with narrative form in order to show the interrelationship of the conscious and unconscious mind. The situation involves a nameless narrator in whose personal history we are only marginally concerned and whose personal future is unimportant. The novel uses elements from the experiential world of the conscious mind and from the mythic world of the unconscious mind in order to present the interdependence and interpenetration of the objective and the subjective, the personal and the transpersonal, the individual and the collective. The mystic belief in cosmic evolution is most clearly articulated in this work. Against a background of social confusion and collapse, the narrator and her alter-ego move into another realm of being.

Each of Lessing's major novels presents its own challenges to the critic, both in terms of form and content. She confronts our conditioned ideas about personality, violence, reality, and progress. Her works all have, as a common thread, the idea of the individual seeking an epistemological basis for the self, but increasingly the person as a unique individual is absent from Lessing's work. She suggests that we are all parts of a larger Self and our breakdowns and maladjustments are merely microcosmic reflections of cultural fragmentation and disorder. Lessing is a humanist because of her genuine love for the individual human, but in her current emphasis the survival of that individual is dependent upon social evolution.

---

1. Minda Bikman, "A Talk with Doris Lessing," *The New York Times Book Review*, 30 March 1980, p. 26.

2. Harry Tayler, brother of Doris Lessing, in an interview with Dee Seligman in February 1973. A much longer interview with Mr. Tayler and several friends of Doris Lessing's appears in *Modern Fiction Studies*, Spring 1980 issue.

3. Michael Thorpe, *Doris Lessing's Africa* (London: Evans Brothers, 1978), p. 11.

4. Bikman, "A Talk with Doris Lessing," p. 25.

5. Malcolm Page, "Lessing's Unpublished Plays," *Doris Lessing Newsletter* 1 (Fall 1977), 6.

6. Claire Sprague, "Introduction to Doris Lessing's *Reasoner* Letters," *Doris Lessing Newsletter* 3 (Summer 1979), 6.

7. Arnold Wesker, "Interview" in *Theatre at Work*, ed. Charles Marowitz and Simon Trussler (New York: Hill and Wang, 1967), p. 86.

8. Page, "Lessing's Unpublished Plays," p. 6.

9. Doris Lessing, "A Plea for the Paperback," *The Guardian*, 3 July 1972, p. 10.

Section I
WORKS BY LESSING

NOVELS

1. The Grass is Singing
    London: Michael Joseph, 1950. Reprinted in 1972.
    New York: T. Y. Crowell, 1950.
    Harmondsworth: Penguin, 1961. Reprinted in 1974.
    New York: Ballantine Books, 1964.
    London: Heinemann, 1973.
    New York: T. Y. Crowell, 1975.

2. Martha Quest (Children of Violence, Vol. I)
    London: Michael Joseph, 1952.
    New York: Simon and Schuster, 1964.
    New York: New American Library, 1964.
    London: Panther Books, 1966.
    New York: Simon and Schuster, 1967.
    St. Albans, Hertfordshire: Hart-Davis, MacGibbon, 1977.
    St. Albans, Hertfordshire: Panther, 1977.

3. A Proper Marriage (Children of Violence, Vol. II)
    London: Michael Joseph, 1954.
    New York: Simon and Schuster, 1964.
    London: Panther Books, 1966.
    New York: New American Library, 1970.
    St. Albans, Hertfordshire: Hart-Davis, MacGibbon, 1977.
    St. Albans, Hertfordshire: Panther Books, 1977.

4. Retreat to Innocence
    London: Michael Joseph, 1956.
    New York: Prometheus Books, 1959.
    London: Sphere, 1967.

5. A Ripple from the Storm (Children of Violence, Vol. III)
    London: Michael Joseph, 1958.
    New York: Simon and Schuster, 1966.
    New York: New American Library, 1970.
    St. Albans, Hertfordshire: Hart-Davis, MacGibbon, 1977.
    St. Albans, Hertfordshire: Panther Books, 1977.

6. The Golden Notebook
    London: Michael Joseph, 1962.
    New York: Simon and Schuster, 1962.
    New York: McGraw Hill, 1963.
    Harmondsworth: Penguin Books, 1964.
    New York: Ballantine Books, 1968.
    London: Michael Joseph, 1972 (new edition with author's
    preface.)
    New York: Bantam Books, 1973 (includes author's
    preface.)
    St. Albans, Hertfordshire: Panther Books, 1973.

7. Landlocked (Children of Violence, Vol. IV)
    London: MacGibbon and Kee, 1965.
    New York: Simon and Schuster, 1966.

New York: New American Library, 1966.
London: Panther Books, 1967.
St. Albans, Hertfordshire: Hart—MacGibbon, 1977.
St. Albans, Hertfordshire: Panther Books, 1977.

8. The Four-Gated City (Children of Violence, Vol. V)
London: MacGibbon and Kee, 1969.
New York: Alfred A. Knopf, 1969.
New York: Bantam Books, 1970
St. Albans, Hertfordshire: Panther Books, 1972.
New York: New American Library, 1976.
St. Albans, Herftordshire: Hart—Davis, MacGibbon, 1977.

9. Briefing for a Descent into Hell
London: Jonathan Cape, 1971.
New York: Alfred A. Knopf, 1971.
New York: Bantam Books, 1972.
St. Albans, Hertfordshire: Panther Books, 1973.

10. The Summer Before the Dark
London: Jonathan Cape, 1973.
New York: Alfred A. Knopf, 1973.
Harmondsworth: Penguin, 1975.

11. The Memoirs of a Survivor
London: Octagon Press, 1974.
New York: Alfred A. Knopf, 1975.
New York: Bantam Books, 1976.
Unpublished typescripts of this novel are in Special
Collections of the McFarlin Library, University of Tulsa,
Tulsa, Oklahoma.

SHORT STORY COLLECTIONS

12. This Was the Old Chief's Country
London: Michael Joseph, 1951.
New York: T. Y. Crowell, 1952.

13. Five: Short Novels
London: Michael Joseph, 1953.
Harmondsworth: Penguin Books, 1960.
St. Albans, Hertfordshire: Panther Books, 1969.

14. The Habit of Loving
London: MacGibbon and Kee, 1957.
New York: Ballantine Books, 1957.
New York: T. Y. Crowell, 1957.
New York: Popular Library, 1957.
Harmondsworth: Penguin Books, 1960.
New York: Ballantine Books, 1965.
London: MacGibbon and Kee, 1966.
St. Albans, Hertfordshire: Hart—Davis, MacGibbon, 1978.
St. Albans, Hertfordshire: Panther Books, 1978.

15. A Man and Two Women
    London: MacGibbon and Kee, 1963.
    New York: Simon and Schuster, 1963.
    New York: Popular Library, 1963.
    London: Panther Books, 1972.
    St. Albans, Hertfordshire: Hart-Davis, MacGibbon, 1978.
    St. Albans, Hertfordshire: Panther Books, 1978.

16. African Stories
    London: Michael Joseph, 1964 (with author's preface.)
    New York: Simon and Schuster, 1965.
    New York: Ballantine Books, 1966.

17. The Black Madonna
    London: Panther Books, 1966.
    St. Albans, Hertfordshire: Panther, 1974.

18. Winter in July
    London: Panther Books, 1966.
    St. Albans, Hertfordshire: Panther Books, 1974.

19. Nine African Stories. Ed. Michael Marland. (with author's
    introduction.)
    London: Longman, 1968.

20. The Temptation of Jack Orkney and Other Stories
    (published in England as The Story of a Non-
    Marrying Man and Other Stories.)
    London: Jonathan Cape, 1972.
    New York: Alfred A. Knopf, 1972.
    New York: Bantam Books, 1974.
    Harmondsworth: Penguin, 1975.
    London: Jonathan Cape, 1978.

21. This Was the Old Chief's Country, Vol. I of Doris
    Lessing's Collected African Stories
    London: Michael Joseph, 1973 (with a new author's
    preface.)
    St. Albans, Hertfordshire: Panther Books, 1979.

22. The Sun Between Their Feet, Vol. II of Doris
    Lessing's Collected African Stories
    London: Michael Joseph, 1973 (with a new author's
    preface.)
    St. Albans, Hertfordshire: Penguin Books, 1979.

23. Sunrise on the Veld
    Cambridge: Cambridge University Press, 1975.

24. A Mild Attack of Locusts
    Cambridge: Cambridge University Press, 1977.

25. To Room Nineteen/Her Collected Stories, Vol. I
    London: Jonathan Cape, 1978.

26. The Temptation of Jack Orkney/Her Collected Stories,
    Vol. II
    London: Jonathan Cape, 1978.
      Unpublished typescripts of this novel are in Special
      Collections of the McFarlin Library, University of
      Tulsa, Tulsa, Oklahoma.

27. Stories
    New York: Alfred A. Knopf, 1978.

SHORT STORIES IN PERIODICALS

28. "The Pig." Trek, 12 (April 1948), 16-17.

29. "Fruit from Ashes," Trek, 13 (October 1949), 14-15.

30. "Flight." Trek, 15 (April 1951),4-7.

31. "Traitors." Argosy, (May 1954), page numbers unavailable.

32. "A Mild Attack of Locusts." New Yorker, 31 (26 February
    1955), 76-83.

33. "Through the Tunnel." New Yorker, 31 (6 August 1955),
    60-70.

34. "Our Friend Judith." Partisan Review, 27 (Summer 1960),
    459-479.

35. "Homage for Isaac Babel." New Statesman, 62 (15 December
    1961), 920+.

36. "From the Black Notebook." Partisan Review, 29 (Spring
    1962), 196-214. Appeared later as part of The Golden
    Notebook.

37. "The New Man." New Statesman, 64 (7 September 1962),
    282-283.

38. "One Off the Short List." Kenyon Review, 25 (Spring 1963),
    217-244.

39. "Letter from Home." Partisan Review, 30 (Summer 1963),
    192-201.

40. "A Room." New Statesman, 66 (2 August 1963), 138-139.

41. "Particularly Cats." McCalls, 94 (March 1967), 110-111.
    Reprinted in Cat Fancy, 12 (March-April 1969 and June
    1969), 49-56. Excerpts from Lessing's work of the same
    title.

42. "Side Benefits of an Honorable Profession," Partisan
    Review, 35 (Fall 1968), 507-518.

43. "Report on the Threatened City." Playboy, 17 (November 1971), 108-110, 250-254, 256, 258, 260, 262.

44. "Spies I Have Known." Partisan Review, 38 (1971), 50-66.

SHORT STORIES IN OTHER COLLECTIONS

45. "The Nuisance." In Towards the Sun: A Miscellany of Southern Africa. Ed. Roy Macnab. London: Collins, 1950, 29-35.

46. "The Black Madonna." Winter's Tales 3. London: MacMillan, 1957, 132-156.

47. "The De Wets Come to Kloof Grange." South African Stories. Ed. David Wright. London: Farber and Farber, 1960, 98-126.

48. "In Pursuit of the English." In Alienation. Ed. Timothy O'Keefe. London: MacGibbon and Kee, 1960, 23-50. Selected from Lessing's work of the same title.

49. "Through the Tunnel." In Great Stories from the World of Sports. Ed. Peter Schwed and Herbert W. Wind. London: Heinemann, 1960, 130-138. Also in Sixteen Stories by South African Writers. Ed. Clive Millar. CapeTown: Maskew Miller, 1964, 123-133. Also in Breath of Danger: Fifty Tales of Peril and Fear by Masters of the Short Story. Ed. Eric Duthie. London: Odhams, 1967, 296-305.

50. "Flight. In Short Stories from Southern Africa. Ed. A. G. Hooper. CapeTown: Oxford University Press, 1963, 85-90.

51. "A Mild Attack of Locusts." In Short Stories from Southern Africa. Ed. A. G. Hooper. CapeTown: Oxford University Press, 1963, 91-98.

52. "Mrs. Fortescue." Winter's Tales 9. Ed. A. D. MacLean. New York: St. Martin's Press, 1963, 149-169.

53. "A Sunrise on the Veld." Sixteen Stories by South African Writers. Ed. Clive Millar. CapeTown: Maskew Miller, 1964, 1-10.

54. "An Unposted Love Letter." In Thy Neighbor's Wife: Twelve Original Variations on a Theme. Ed. James Turner. London: Cassell, 1964, 81-91.

55. Black and White in Africa: Three Stories. Ed. Kurt
    Schrey. Frankfurt: Mortiz Diesteiweg, 1965. Includes
    "The Old Chief Mshlanga;" "No Witchcraft for Sale;"
    "Little Tembi."

56. "Little Tembi." In Modern Choice I. Ed. Eva Figes.
    London: Blackie, 1965, 61-94.

57. "To Room Nineteen." In The World of Modern Fiction:
    European. Ed. Stephen Marcus. New York: Simon and
    Schuster, 1966, 262-291.

58. "Two Boys." In Modern African Narrative.
    Ed. Paul Edwards. London: Nelson, 1966, 124-139. An
    excerpt from "The Antheap."

59. "The Antheap." In Great British Short Novels.
    Ed. R. D. Spector. New York: Bantam, 1971, 129-183.

60. "An Old Woman and Her Cat." New American Review 14.
    Ed. Theodore Solotaroff. New York: Simon and Schuster,
    1972, 68-84.

61. "A Woman on a Roof." In Loves, Hopes, and Fears.
    Ed. Michael Marland. London: Longman Imprint, 1975.

62. "The Words He Said." In Friends and Families.
    Ed. Eileen and Michael Marland. London: Longman
    Imprint, 1973.

63. Catell, Alan. Doris Lessing. London: Harrap and Co.,
    1976. The stories collected here are "Story of Two
    Dogs"; "Traitors"; "Homage for Isaac Babel"; "No
    Witchcraft for Sale"; "An Old Woman and Her Cat"; "Story of
    a Non-Marrying Man"; "A Woman on a Roof"; "Outside the
    Ministry"; "England vs. England"; "Out of
    the Fountain"; and "Notes for a Case History."
    This is a school text edition of these stories and includes
    questions for discussion.

PLAYS

64. Mr. Dolinger. Unpublished play. Produced 7 July 1958
    at the Oxford Playhouse. For description see John
    Russell Taylor, The Angry Theater: New British Drama.
    New York: Hill and Wang, 1969, 145. Also see Myron
    Matlaw, Modern World Drama: An Encyclopedia. New York:
    E. P. Dutton and Co., 1972, 456.

65. Each His Own Wilderness. In New English Dramatists,
    Three Plays. Ed. E. Martin Browne. Harmondsworth,
    Middlesex: Penguin Books, 1959. Also in The Long and
    the Tall and Each His Own Wilderness. Ed. Willis Hall.
    Harmondsworth, Middlesex: Penguin, 1968.

66. The Truth About Billy Newton. Unpublished play.   Produced
    18 January 1960 at Salisbury Arts Theater, Salisbury,
    Wiltshire, England. For description see Allardyce Nicoll,
    "Somewhat in a New Dimension." In Contemporary Theater,
    Stratford-Upon-Avon-Studies 4.
    London: Edward Arnold Publishers Ltd., 1968, 82-83, 92.

67. Play with a Tiger: A Play in Three Acts.
    London: Michael Joseph, 1962.
    London: Daivs-Poyner Ltd., 1972.
    In Plays of the Sixties, Vol. I. Ed. J. M. Charlton.
    London: Pan Books, 1966. Includes postscript by Lessing.
    Also in Plays by and about Women. Ed. Victoria
    Sullivan and James Hatch. New York: Random House, 1973,
    201-275.

POEMS

68. "Under My Hand." Trek, 13 (February 1949), 25.

69. "Plea for the Hated Dead Woman." New Statesman, 51 (30
    June 1955), 768.

70. Fourteen Poems. Northwood, Middlesex: Scorpion Press,
    1959.

71. "Here." New Statesman, 71 (17 June 1966), 900.

72. "A Visit." New Statesman, 72 (4 November 1966), 666.

73. "Small Girl Throws Stones at a Swan in Regents Park;"
    "Hunger the King." New Statesman, 74 (24 November
    1967), 731.

74. "The Song of a Bourgeois;" "Fable." Excerpted in
    Zambezia: The Journal of the University of Rhodesia,
    6 (1978), 211.

AUTOBIOGRAPHICAL NARRATIVES

75. "Myself as Sportsman." New Yorker, 31 (21 January 1956),
    92-96.

76. "Being Prohibited." New Statesman, 51 (21 April 1956),
    410-412.

77. Going Home
    London: Michael Joseph, 1957. Drawings by Paul Hogarth.
    London: Panther Books, 1968. Revised edition.
    New York: Ballantine Books, 1968. Revised edition.
    St. Albans, Hertfordshire: Panther Books, 1968.
    Revised edition.

78. Omitted.

79. In Pursuit of the English: A Documentary.
    London: MacGibbon and Kee, 1960.
    New York: Simon and Schuster, 1961.
    London: Mayflower, 1961.
    London: Sphere, 1968.
    New York: Ballantine Books, 1966.
    St. Albans, Hertfordshire: Hart-Davis, MacGibbon, 1978.

80. "All Seething Underneath." Vogue, (15 February 1964),
    80-81; 132-133.
        First appeared as "My Father." London Sunday
    Telegraph, 1 September 1963. Also in A Small Personal
    Voice. Ed. Paul Schlueter.
    New York: Alfred A. Knopf, 1974, 83-93.

81. Particularly Cats.
    London: Michael Joseph, 1967.
    New York: Simon and Schuster, 1967.
    New York: New American Library, 1971.
    New York: Simon and Schuster, 1978.

ESSAYS

82. Rhodesian Friends of the Soviet Union Magazine. 1943. (?)
    Available from the National Archives of Rhodesia.
    Lessing wrote articles for this publication during
    World War II.

83. "The Small Personal Voice." In Declaration. Ed. Tom
    Maschler. London: MacGibbon and Kee, 1957.

84. "Ordinary People." New Statesman, 59 (25 June 1960),   932.

85. "What Really Matters." Twentieth Century, 172 (Autumn
    1963), 96-98.

86. "Omar Khayyam." New Statesman, 74 (15 December 1967),   847.

87. "An Ancient Way to New Freedom." Vogue, 158 (15 September
    1971), 98, 125, 130-131. Also in The
    Diffusion of Sufi Ideas in the West. Ed. L. Lewin.
    Boulder: Keysign Press, 1972.

88. "The Education of Doris Lessing." Observer Supplement,
    26 September 1971, 53-55. (illustrated).

89. "In the World, Not of It." Encounter, 39 (August 1972),
    61-64. Also in A Small Personal Voice. Ed.
    Paul Schlueter. New York: Alfred A. Knopf, 1974, 129-139.

90. "On the Golden Notebook." Partisan Review, 40 (Winter
    1973), 14-30. Also in A Small Personal Voice. Ed. Paul
    Schlueter. New York: Alfred A. Knopf, 1974, 23-45.

91. A Small Personal Voice. Ed. Paul Schlueter.
    New York: Alfred A. Knopf, 1974.
    New York: Vintage, 1975.

92. "If You Knew Sufi." The Guardian, 8 January 1975, 12.

93. "A Revolution." New York Times, 22 August 1975, 31.

> Interesting comments by Lessing on the Western
> world's ignorance of Islamic culture and its
> historical contributions. She particularly
> chafes at our ignorance of Idries Shah, the
> Sufi teacher, who is celebrated in a
> Festschrift she mentions. She acknowledges her
> own belief in the potential conscious evolution
> of the human race.

94. "Building a New Cultural Understanding with the People
    of the East." The Times (London), 15 October 1975, 8.

REPORTAGE

95. Minutes of the Congress of the African Branch of the
    Southern Rhodesian Labour Party held at Jabula Hall,
    Harare on 12 February 1944. Available from National
    Archives of Rhodesia.

> Lessing acted as secretary of this meeting; the
> meeting is of historical importance when reading
> A Ripple from the Storm.

96. "Kariba Project." New Statesman, 51 (9 June 1956),
    647-648.

97. "London Diary." New Statesman, 55 (15 March 1958),
    326-327.

98. "London Diary." New Statesman, 55 (22 March 1958),
    367-368.

99. "Crisis in Central Africa: the Fruits of Humbug."
    Twentieth Century, 165 (April 1959), 368-376.

100. "Smart Set Socialists." New Statesman, 62 (1 December 1961), 822, 824.

101. "Zambia's Joyful Week." New Statesman, 68 (6 November 1964), 692, 694.

102. "A Few Doors Down." New Statesman, 78 (26 December 1968), 918-919.

103. Omitted

BOOK REVIEWS

104. "Desert Child." New Statesman, 56 (15 November 1958), 700.

     Review of Laurens Van Der Post's The Lost World of the Kalaheri.

105. "African Interiors." New Statesman, 62 (27 October 1961), 613-614.

     Review of Laurens Van Der Post's The Heart of the Hunter.

106. "An Elephant in the Dark." Spectator, 213 (18 September 1964), 373.

     Review of Idries Shah's The Sufis.

107. African-English Literature. Ed. Anne Tibble. London: Peter Owen, 1965, 52, 296.

     Quotes Lessing's comments on Alfred Hutchinson's novel, Road to Ghana.

108. "Allah Be Praised." New Statesman, 71 (27 May 1966), 775.

     Review of Malcolm X's Autobiography. Reprinted in A Small Personal Voice. Ed. Paul Schlueter. New York: Alfred A. Knopf, 1974, 121-129.

109. "Afterword." The Story of an African Farm. (New York: Fawcett World Library, 1968), 273-290.

     Reprinted as "Introduction." The Story of an African Farm. (New York: Schocken Books, 1976), 1-18. Also reprinted in A Small Personal Voice, 97-121.

110. "A Deep Darkness." New Statesman, (15 January 1971),
     87-88.

     Review of Isak Dinesin (Karen Blixen's) Shadows on
     the Grass and Out of Africa. Reprinted in
     A Small Personal Voice, 147-155.

111. "Ant's Eye View." New Statesman, 81 (29 January 1971),
     149-150.

     Review of Eugene Marais's The Soul of the White Ant.
     Reprinted in A Small Personal Voice, 143-147.

112. "What Looks Like an Egg and is an Egg?" New York Times
     Book Review, 77 (7 May 1972), 6, 41-43.

     Lessing discusses Sufism.

113. "Foreword." In An Ill-Fated People, Zimbabwe Before
     and After Rhodes by Lawrence Vambe. London: Heinemann,
     1972, xii-xxi. Also published by Pittsburgh:
     University of Pittsburgh Press, 1973, xii-xxi.

114. "Vonnegut's Responsibility." New York Times Book Review,
     (4 February 1973), 35.

     Review of Vonnegut's Mother Night. Reprinted in A
     Small Personal Voice, 139-143.

115. Review of The Inner World of Mental Illness. Ed. Bert
     Kaplan. New York Times Book Review, 23 September 1973,
     16-18.

116. "The Ones Who Know." Times Literary Supplement, 3868
     (30 April 1976), 514-515.

     Review of six books on Sufism. Lessing finds Sufism
     unbound by any particular culture and unaffiliated
     with any religious dogma.

LETTERS

117. Unmailed letter to The Rhodesia Herald, 15 December 1945.
     Available from the National Archives of
     Rhodesia. SR 1/4/3 Policy, January 1938-December
     1947; General, February 1944-December 1947.

     This document is useful as an historical reference
     point on the events of the Gwelo Congress depicted
     in A Ripple from the Storm. See "Children of
     Violence and Rhodesia: A Study of Doris Lessing as
     Historical Observer," Ed. M. C. Steele. (Salisbury:
     Central African Historical Association, 1974), 21.

118. "Letter to the Editor." New Statesman, 12 (3 November 1961), 651.

119. "Sex and the Turning Worm." The Guardian, 8 January 1969, 8.

120. "Letter to the Editor." New York Review of Books, 15 22 October 1970), 51.

121. "A Plea for the Paperback." The Guardian 3 July 1972, 10.

> Lessing urges newspapers to review paperbacks in order to encourage publishers to print new books in paperback form. An expression of her own desire to put her work into the hands of the general public and not just that affluent few.

122. Letters to Roberta Rubenstein. 17 November 1972, 31 December 1972, 11 January 1977, 28 March 1977. Excerpted in Rubenstein's The Novelistic Vision of Doris Lessing (Urbana: University of Illinois, 1979).

123. Sprague, Claire. "Doris Lessing's Reasoner Letters." Doris Lessing Newsletter, 3 (Summer 1979), 6-8.

> Two letters written by Lessing to The Reasoner, a Communist Party publication which appeared after the 1956 Twentieth Party Congress. These letters have not been repinted elsewhere and provide evidence of the extent of Lessing's involvement in Party problems and language at this time.

TAPE RECORDINGS

124. "An Ancient Way to New Freedom." Part of series, "The
     Traditional Psychologies" for Seminar Cassettes Ltd., 218
     Sussex Gardens, London W2 3UD, England.

125. "An Interview with Doris Lessing." Pacific Tape
     Library, 1963. BB3368. 47 minute cassette.

126. "Doris Lessing Reads Her Short Stories." New York:
     Jeffrey Norton, 1974, 23182. 1 cassette.

     Recorded at the Poetry Center of the YM-YWHA in New
     York on 15 May 1969.

127. WBAI Radio interview by Josephine Hendin, New York, New
     York . Unpublished.

     Recorded 30 December 1972.

128. "The Works of Doris Lessing." Tape by Virginia Tiger on
     Lessing. Everett Edwards, Inc., P.O. Box 1060,
     Deland, Fla. 32720. #5521.

129. Unpublished radio interviews with Studs Terkel. 10 June
     1969; 8 October 1970.

TELEVISION SCRIPTS

130. "Care and Protection." Independent Television Series,
     "Blackmail," London (30 September 1966).

131. "Do Not Disturb." Independent Television Series,
     "Blackmail," London 25 (November 1966).

     Lessing describes these pieces in "A Conversation
     with Doris Lessing," (Florence Howe interview).
     In Doris Lessing: Critical Studies. Ed. Annis
     Pratt and L. S. Dembo. (Madison: University of
     Wisconsin Press, 1974, 18-19.

THEATER CRITICISM

132. "Freud Amond the Teacups." The Observer, 9 November
     1958, 19.

133. "The Living Pat." The Observer, 16 November 1958, 19.

134. "Two Brands of Corn." The Observer, 23 November 1958, 17.

135. "The Dusseldorf Monster." <u>The Observer</u>, 30 November 1958, 17.

136. "A Time for Rebellion." <u>The Observer</u>, 7 December 1958, 15.

Section II
TRANSLATIONS
OF LESSING'S WORKS

BELGIUM

137. Het Zingende Gras (The Grass is Singing).
     Trans. Paul van Kampen.
     Antwerp: Martens and Stappaerts, 1953.

CHILE

138. Regreso a la Inocencia (Retreat to Innocence).
     Trans. Carmen Cienfuegos.
     Santiago: Zig-Zag, 1969.

CUBA

139. Canta la Hierba (The Grass is Singing).
     Trans. Jose Maria Valverde.
     Havana: Instituto del Libro, 1969.

CZECHOSLOVAKIA

140. Africke Povidky (stories from This Was the Old Chief's
     Country and The Habit of Loving).
     Trans. Petr Pujman.
     Prague: Statni Nakladatelstvi Krasne Literatury
     a Umeni, 1961.

141. Mraveniště (stories from Five and The Habit of Loving)
     Trans. Olga Fialova, Wanda Zamecka, Zora Wolfova.
     Prague: Mlada Fronta, 1961.

142. Hra S. Tygrem (Play with a Tiger).
     Trans. Jiři Mucha.
     Prague: Dilia, 1966.

143. Muž a Dvě Ženy (stories from A Man and Two Women).
     Trans. Zora Wolfova.
     Prague: Mlada Fronta, 1970.

144. Tráva Zpíva (The Grass is Singing).
     Trans. Jři Valja.
     Praha: Práce, 1974.

145. Tráva Spieva (The Grass is Singing).
     Trans. Gabriela Hanákova
     Bratislava: Slov, 1974.

DENMARK

146. Graesset Synger (The Grass is Singing).
     Trans. Hagmund Hansen.
     Copenhagen: Fremad, 1952.

147. Vinter I Juli (Winter in July).
     Trans. Hedda Løvlad.
     Copenhagen: Aschehoug, 1957.

148. Graesset Synger (The Grass is Singing).
     Trans. Hagmund Hansen.
     Copenhagen: Fremad, 1969.

149. Sommaren før Mørket (The Summer Before the Dark).
     Trans. Merete Ries.
     Copenhagen: Gyldendal, 1974.

150. Den Gyldne Bog (The Golden Notebook).
     Trans. Merete Ries.
     Copenhagen: Gyldendal, 1975.

151. En Overlevendes Erindringer (The Memoirs of a
     Survivor).
     Trans. Merete Ries.
     Copenhagen: Gyldendal, 1975.

FINLAND

152. Kultainen Muistrikirja (The Golden Notebook).
     Trans. Eeva Siikarla.
     Helsinki: Werner Söderström, 1968.

153. Sommaren Före Morkret (The Summer Before the Dark).
     Trans. Sonja Bergvall.
     Helsinfors: Söderström, 1973.

154. Kesä Ennen Pimeää (The Summer Before the Dark).
     Trans. Irmeli Sallamo.
     Helsinki: Kirjayhtymä, 1974.

155. Unesta Päivää (Briefing for a Descent into Hell).
     Trans. Irmeli Sallamo.
     Helsingki: Kirjayhtma, 1973.

156. En Överlevandes Minnen (The Memoirs of a Survivor).
     Trans. Sonja Bergvall.
     Helsinfors: Söderström, 1975.

FRANCE

157. Vaincue par la Brousse (The Grass is Singing).
     Trans. Doussia Ergaz.
     Paris: Plon, 1953.

158. Les Enfants de la Violence (1): Martha Quest
     (Children of Violence, Martha Quest).
     Trans. Doussia Ergaz and Florence Cravoisier.
     Paris: Plon, 1957.

159. "Sa Petite Voix Personnelle," en Les Jeunes Gens
     en Colere vous Parlent ("A Small Personal Voice"
     in Declaration), 7-30.
     Trans. Michel Chrestien.
     Paris: P. Horay, 1958.

160. Un Homme, Deux Femmes (stories from A Man and
     Two Women).
     Trans. Jacqueline Marc-Chadourne.
     Paris: Plon, 1967.

161. Le Carnet d'Or.
     Trans. Marianne Véron
     Paris: Albin Michel, 1976.

162. Les Enfants de la Violence (Children of Violence)
     Trans: Unknown
     Paris: Albin Michel, 1978.

GERMANY

163. Afrikanische Tragödie (The Grass is Singing).
     Trans. Ernst Sander.
     Gütersloh: Bertelsmann, 1953.

164. Die Andere Frau ("The Other Woman").
     Trans. Ernst Sander.
     Gütersloh: Bertelsmann, 1954.

165. Der Zauber ist Nicht Verkäuflich
     (stories from Five and This Was the Old Chief's
     Country).
     Trans. Lore Kruger.
     Berlin: Tribune, 1956.

166. Der Sommer vor der Dunkelheit (The Summer Before
     the Dark).
     Trans. Jürgen Abel.
     Reinbek (bei Hamburg): Rowolhlt, 1975.

167. Das Goldene Notizbuch (The Golden Notebook)
Trans. Iris Wagner
Frankfurt: Goverts, 1978.

168. Erzählung (Hunger)
Trans. Lore Krüger
Zurich: Diogenes Zürich/VVA, 1976.

HUNGARY

169. Eldorádó: Elbeszélesék (Five: Short Novels).
Trans. Tibor Bartos.
Budapest: Uj Magyar Kiadó, 1956.

ITALY

170. L'erba Canta (The Grass is Singing).
Trans. Maria Stella Ferrari.
Rome: Casini, 1952.

171. La Noia di Essere Moglie: Romanzo (A Proper
Marriage).
Trans. Fracesco Saba Sardi.
Milan: Feltrinelli, 1957.

172. A Ciascuno il suo Deserto (Each His Own Wilderness).
Trans. Liciano Codignola.
Turin: Einaudi, 1963.

173. Il Taccuino D'Oro (The Golden Notebook).
Trans. Maria Rivia Serini.
Milan: Feltrinelli, 1964.

174. Commedia con la Tigre (Play with a Tiger).
Trans. Maria Rivia Serini.
Turin: Einaudi, 1967.

175. La Noia di Essere Moglie: Romanzo (A Proper
Marriage).
Trans. Fracesco Saba Sardi.
Milan: Feltrinelli, 1967.

176. L'estate Prima del Buio (The Summer Before the Dark).
Trans. Tullio Dobner.
Milan: Bompiani, 1974.

JAPAN

177. Kusa wa Utatte Irv (The Grass is Singing).
Trans. Yamazaki Tsutomu and Sakai Tadashi.
Tokyo: Shôbunsha, 1970.

178. Translation of The Summer Before the Dark.
Trans. Yamazaki Tsutomu.
Tokyo: Shobunsha, date unknown.

LATVIA

179. Burvestiba Nav Pardodama (stories from This Was the
Old Chief's Country and Five).
Trans. Z. Stava.
Riga: Latgosizdat, 1961.

NETHERLANDS

180. Het Zingende Gras (The Grass is Singing).
Trans. Paul van Kampen.
Amsterdam: G. W. Breughel, 1953.

> Reprinted in 1974 by Contact Press (same
> translator).

181. Een Man En Twee Vrouwen (stories from A Man and
Two Women).
Trans. P. Van Vliet.
Amsterdam: J. M. Meulenhof, 1965.

182. Pas Op Jezelf, Lieveling (stories from A Man and
Two Women).
Trans. P. van Vliet.
Amsterdam: J. M. Meulenhof, 1966.

183. De Zomer voor het Donker (The Summer Before
the Dark).
Trans. Netty Vink.
Amsterdam: Contact, 1974.

NORWAY

184. Det Synger i Gresset (The Grass is Singing).
Trans. Eli Krog.
Stavanger: Stabenfeldt, 1951.

> Reprinted in Oslo: Gyldendal, 1975.

185. Sommeren før Mørket (The Summer Before the Dark).
     Trans. Moha Lange.
     Oslo: Gyldendal, 1974.

186. Den Gyldne Notatbok (The Golden Notebook).
     Trans. Mona Lange.
     Oslo: Pax, 1975.

187. En Overlevendes Erindringer (The Memoirs of a
     Survivor).
     Trans. Torborg Nedreass.
     Oslo: Gyldendal, 1975.

POLAND

188. Mrowisko (Five: Short Stories).
     Trans. Agnieszka Glinczanka.
     Warsaw: Pánstw. Instytut Wydawn., 1956.

189. Pokoj Nr 19 (stories from A Man and Two Women).
     Trans. Waclaw Niepokólczycki.
     Warsaw: Pánstw. Instytut. Wydawn., 1966.

PORTUGAL

190. A Erva Canta (The Grass is Singing).
     Trans. Daniel Goncalves.
     Lisbon: Ulisseia, 1964.

191. O Verão Antes das Trevas (The Summer Before the Dark).
     Trans. Fernanda P. Rodrigues.
     Lisbon: Livros do Brasil, 1974.

RUMANIA

192. Cealalta Femeie (stories from Five).
     Trans. Mircea Alexandrescu.
     Bucharest: Editua de Stat Pentru Literatura si
         Arta, 1958.

RUSSIA

193. Muravejnik ("The Antheap").
     Trans. S. Terehina and I. Manenok.
     Moscow: Pravda, 1956.

194. No Witchcraft for Sale: Stories and Short Novels.
     Moscow: Foreign Languages Publishing House, 1956.

195. Omitted.

196. Marta Kvest (Martha Quest).
     Trans. T. A. Kudrjavcera.
     Moscow: Izdatelstvo, 1957.

197. Imerohi Ei Ole Müüdav Ja Teisi Jutte (stories from
     This was the Old Chief's Country).
     Trans. V. Rand.
     Tallinn: Gaz.-Zurn.-izd., 1957.

198. Povesti (stories from This was the Old Chief's Country
     and Five).
     Trans. A. Ljubovcov et. al.
     Moscow: Izdatelstvo, 1958.

199. Naš Sekret Ne Prodaetsja (stories from Five and
     This Was the Old Chief's Country).
     Trans. M. Selija.
     Tiflis: Nakaduli, 1963.

SPAIN

200. La Costumbre de Amar (The Habit of Loving).
     Trans. Maria Luisa Borras.
     Barcelona: Seix Barral, 1964.

201. Un Hombre y Dos Mujeres (A Man and Two Women).
     Trans. Georgina Regás
     Barcelona: Seix Barral, 1967.

202. Canta La Hierba (The Grass is Singing).
     Trans. Jose M. Valverde.
     Barcelona: Seix Barral, 1968.

203. Martha Quest
     Trans. Francesc Parcerisas.
     Barcelona: Seix Barral, 1973.

204. Instrucciones para un Viaje al Infierno (Briefing
     for a Descent into Hell).
     Trans. Manuel Villas.
     Barcelona: Seix Barral, 1974.

205. El Último Verano de Mrs. Brown (The Summer Before the
     Dark).
     Trans. Francesc Parcerisas.
     Barcelona: Seix Barral, 1974.

SWEDEN

206. Gräset Sjunder (The Grass is Singing).
     Trans. Gunvor Hökby and Bertil Hökby.
     Stockholm: Hökerberg, 1951.

207. Flickan Martha (Martha Quest).
     Trans. Gunnar Frösell.
     Stockholm: Hökerberg, 1953.

208. Den Femte Sanningen (The Golden Notebook).
     Trans. Mårten Edlund.
     Stockholm: Forum, 1964.

     Reprinted in 1970 in two volumes.

209. En Man Och Trå Krinnor (stories from A Man and
     Two Women).
     Trans. Harriet Alfons and Jadwiga P. Westrup.
     Stockholm: Forum, 1965.

210. Vanan Att Älska (stories from The Habit of Loving
     and A Man and Two Women).
     Trans. Harriet Alfons and Jadwiga P. Westrup.
     Stockholm: Forum, 1966.

     Reprinted in 1971.

211. Katter (Particularly Cats).
     Trans. Harriet Alfons and Jadwiga P. Westrup.
     Stockholm: Forum, 1968.

212. Ingen Trolldom Till Salv (African Stories).
     Trans. Harriet Alfons and Jadwiga P. Westrup.
     Stockholm: Forum, 1969.

     Reprinted in 1974.

213. Staden Med Frya Portar (The Four-Gated City).
     Trans. Kjell Ekström.
     Stockholm: Forum, 1970.

     Reprinted in 1975 by Trevi.

214. Instruktion För Nedstigning i Helvetet
     (Briefing for a Descent into Hell).
     Trans. Sonja Bergvall.
     Stockholm: Trevi; Solna; Seelig, 1971.

     Reprinted in 1974.

215. En Man Och Två Kvinnor (A Man and Two Women).
     Trans. Harriet Alfons and Jadwiga P. Westrup.
     Stockholm: Forum, 1971.

216. Martha Quest: Del i Serien Valdets Barn (Martha
     Quest: Vol. I, Children of Violence).
     Trans. Sonja Bergvall.
     Stockholm: Trevi, 1972.

     Reprinted in 1975.

217. Inte Den Typ Som Gifter Sig (The Story of a Non-
     Marrying Man).
     Trans. Sonja Bergvall.
     Stockholm: Trevi; Solna; Seelig, 1972.

218. Bra Gift (A Proper Marriage).
     Trans. Sonja Bergvall.
     Stockholm: Trevi, 1973.

     Reprinted in 1975.

219. Sommaren Före Mörkret (The Summer Before the Dark).
     Trans. Sonja Bergvall.
     Stockholm: Trevi, 1973.

     Reprinted in 1975.

220. En Fläkt av Stormen (A Ripple from the Storm).
     Trans. Sonja Bergvall.
     Stockholm: Trevi, 1974.

221. Instängd (Landlocked).
     Trans. Sonja Bergvall.
     Stockholm: Trevi, 1975.

222. En Överlevandes Minnen (The Memoirs of a Survivor).
     Trans. Sonja Bergvall.
     Stockholm: Trevi, 1975.

UNITED ARAB REPUBLIC

223. Al-Tihaw Kullun Fī Baydā'ih (Each His Own Wilderness).
     Trans. Sa'd Zahrān.
     Al-Qāhirah: al-Dār al-Qua mīyah, 1966.

Section III
WORKS ABOUT LESSING

BIOGRAPHY

224. Brewster, Dorothy. <u>Doris Lessing</u>. New York: Twayne Publishers, Inc., 1965, 11-33.

    A good general chapter on Lessing's biography.

225. Godwin, Gail. "The Personal Matter of Doris Lessing." <u>North American Review</u>, 256 (Summer 1971), 66-70.

    A brief discourse on Godwin's own introduction to Lessing's work in the early sixties, and the way in which the work is received by feminists of the seventies. Lessing's personal history is discussed as important to her development as a writer.

226. Harte, Barbara and Caroline Riley, eds. <u>Two Hundred Contemporary Authors: Bio-Bibliographies of Selected Leading Writers of Today with Critical and Personal Sidelights.</u> Detroit: Gale Research, 1969, 162-168.

227. Ichikawa, Hiroyoshi. "Dorisologist or Lessing Freak?" <u>Doris Lessing Newsletter</u>, 1 (Fall 1977), 1, 8-9.

    This personal essay recalls the Japanese professor's attendance at a party given by Doris Lessing.

228. Langley, L. "Scenario for Salvation." <u>Guardian Weekly</u>, 14 April 1971, 8.

    A brief interview which provides a domestic image of the writer, but little new information.

229. Seligman, Dee. "A Visit to Rhodesia." <u>Doris Lessing Newsletter</u>, 1 (Winter 1976), 1, 7.

    This essay describes racial conditions in Rhodesia as observed in 1973. It is derived from the author's dissertation on "The Autobiographical Fiction of Doris Lessing" (see #1012). The chapter in this dissertation which includes interviews with Lessing's Rhodesian relatives and friends appears in <u>Modern Fiction Studies</u>, 25 (Spring 1980).

INTERVIEWS

230. Anonymous. "The Witness as Prophet." Time, 94 (July 25, 1969), 75-76.

      A very brief interview in which Lessing's first visit to the United States (in 1969) is documented.

231. Bannon, Barbara A. "Authors and Editors." Publishers Weekly, 195 (2 June 1969), 51-54.

      An interview with Lessing on the occasion of her 1969 visit. Interesting discussion of her sequential writing even in The Golden Notebook, and in the descipline which writing for T. V. brought her. Short but concise analyses of Lessing on schizophrenia, depression, and E.S.P.

232. Bikman, Minda. "A Talk with Doris Lessing." The New York Times Book Review, 30 March 1980, 1, 24-27.

233. Driver, C. J. "Profile 8: Doris Lessing." The New Review, 1 (November 1974), 17-23.

      An excellent discussion with Lessing of her more recent work. Driver, a Rhodesian, is familiar with her work and offers an interesting analysis of her style as "deliberately clumsy roughening;" which Lessing affirms. He discusses the difference between Lessing as a political ideologue and as a committed writer. Her interest in Sufism is ascribed to certain personal experiences, reading in esoteric literature, and the presence of a practising Sufi teacher (Idries Shah, presumably.) Lessing states that she is not an autobiographical writer because "it is impossible to write autobiographically. Or I've always found it so. You see, I don't think we are as unique as all that ... it's impossible to have an experience that other people haven't had, or aren't having."

234. Ebert, Roger. "Doris Lessing: An Idol on a Mercurial Pedestal." Louisville Courier Journal and Times, 22 June 1969, Sec.G, p. 4, cols. 5-6.

      An interview of Lessing in Chicago during her 1969 U.S. visit. Not too much new information in this brief interview.

235. Haas, Joseph. "Doris Lessing: Chronicler of the
      Cataclysm." Chicago Sun Times, Panorama Magazine,
      14 June 1969, 4-5.

           An interview primarily concerned with Lessing's
           views on madness, E.S.P., nuclear doom, the
           women's movement, and science fiction. Most
           of these opinions have been expressed elsewhere,
           but her comments on leaving the Communist Party
           in 1956 are of particular interest.

236. Howe, Florence. "A Talk with Doris Lessing." The
      Nation, 6 March 1967, 311-313.

           Brief interview from 1966 in which Lessing
           discusses The Golden Notebook. Published in
           lengthier form in Schlueter, A Small Personal
           Voice (#91) and Pratt, Annis and L. Dembo,
           eds., Doris Lessing: Critical Studies. (#254).

237. Howe, Florence. "A Conversation with Doris Lessing
      (1966)." Contemporary Literature, 14 (Autumn 1973),
      418-436.

           This intervieww is required reading for Lessing
           students. Howe discusses The Golden Notebook,
           The Four-Gated City, race relations, Lessing's
           attitude to left-wing politics, and many other
           subjects with Lessing and her son, Peter. A
           respectful and restrained interview, this piece
           nonetheless reveals much about Lessing. Reprinted
           in Schlueter, A Small Personal Voice (#91) and
           Pratt and Dembo, eds., Doris Lessing: Critical
           Studies (#254).

238. Hendin, Josephine. Unpublished interview with Lessing
      on WBAI Radio, New York, New York on 30 December 1972.

239. Newquist, Roy. Counterpoint. New York: Rand McNally
      Co., 1964, 413-424.

           One of the best of the interviews, this piece
           covers such topics as advice to young writers,
           Lessing's childhood in Africa, a comparison of
           the cultural position of writers in the U.S.
           and in England, and a description of her
           mescaline "trip". The latter is fascinating for
           the light it shines on The Golden Notebook.

240. Oates, Joyce Carol. "A Visit with Doris Lessing."
     The Southern Review, 9 (October 1973), 873-883.

     Offers glimpses of Lessing's domestic sur-
     roundings and statements by her concerning
     other writers whom she admires or with whom she
     feels some affinity. Her list includes
     Vonnegut, Norman Mailer, D. H. Lawrence, Saul
     Bellow, Nadine Gordimer, and Margaret Drabble.

241. Raskin, Joseph. "Doris Lessing at Stony Brook." New
     American Review, 8. New York: New American Library,
     1970, 166-179.

     Reprinted in Schlueter, A Small Personal Voice
     (#91).

242. Rubens, Robert. "Footnote to The Golden Notebook."
     The Queen, 21 August 1962, 1962, 31-32.

     A worthwhile interview in which Lessing
     explains her intentions in The Golden Noteboook,
     her absorption with the work of Thomas Mann,
     Patrick Hamilton, and the Russian novelists of
     the nineteenth century. Also Lessing clarifies
     her relation to the English tradition of the
     novel.

243. Terkel, Studs. Unpublished radio interviews. 10 June
     1969; 8 October 1970.

244. WBAI Radio, New York, New York on 8 October, 1963.

245. Wiseman, Thomas. "Mrs. Lessing's Kind of Life."
     Time and Tide, 43 (12 April 1962), 26.

     Good description of Lessing in the early
     sixties. She describes the peculiar situation
     of being an unmarried woman writer and also
     mentions her Jungian therapy.

246. Wyndham, Francis. "The Doors of Perception."
     The Sunday Times (London), 18 November 1979, 41.

BOOK-LENGTH CRITICISM

247. Brewster, Dorothy. Doris Lessing. New York: Twayne
      Publishers, 1965.

        A thorough book for its time, this work now seems
        dated. No thesis is offered to provide an over-
        view of the work, nor is there any systematic
        school of criticism applied. A survey of plot and
        theme is presented of The Grass is Singing, Five,
        the African Stories, A Man and Two Women, Retreat
        to Innocence, the first four volumes of Children
        of Violence (Landlocked was read in typescript),
        and The Golden Notebook. An introductory
        biography of Lessing is helpful, particularly
        because it interweaves known biographical material
        with such personal narratives as In Pursuit of the
        English and Going Home.

248. Schlueter, Paul. The Novels of Doris Lessing.
      Carbondale and Edwardsville: Southern Illinois
      University Press, 1969.

        One of the earliest books on Lessing,
        Schlueter's work does not touch on the Jungian,
        Laingian, Sufist, or mystical orientations which
        predominate in Lessing criticism today. However,
        it is useful as it focuses on her earlier works
        and provides a thematic approach to her work.
        The Grass is Singing, Children of Violence,
        The Golden Notebook, Retreat to Innocence, and
        Briefing for a Descent into Hell are discussed.
        Such themes as the appeal of communism to the lib-
        eral mind, the racial situation of southern
        Africa, the "free woman" in a patriarchal society,
        and the function of writing as therapy provide the
        focuses for these works. The Golden Notebook is
        treated as a summation of Lessing's position, a
        fact which limits the critical breadth of the
        book since Lessing has written other major works
        since then.

249. Steele, M. C. "White Working Class Disunity: The
      Southern Rhodesian Labour Party." Rhodesian History,
      I (1970), 59-81.

        This historical monograph is of interest because
        it sheds light on the polical material in
        A Ripple from the Sotrm. Also compares Steele's
        study on "Lessing as Historical Observer" (#252).

250. Schlueter, Paul. The Fiction of Doris Lessing. Evansville: University of Evansville, 1971.

A collection of papers first presented at the Modern Language Association's seminar on Doris Lessing in 1971 and chaired by Schlueter. The papers included are: Ashley, Leonard R. N. "Children of Violence as a 'Golden Notebook': The Writing of Doris Lessing;" Selma R. "Wholeness as Hieroglyph: Lessing's Typical Mode and Meaning;" Marchino, Lois. "The Search for Self in the Novels of Doris Lessing;" Smith, Diane S. "Ant Imagery as Thematic Device in the Children of Violence Series."

251. Thorpe, Michael. Doris Lessing. British Council for Longman Group, Longman House, Burnt Mill, Harlow, Essex, 1973.

Includes chapters on The Grass is Singing, the African stories, Children of Violence, The Golden Notebook, and Briefing for a Descent into Hell, but not on later stories. The discussion of Marxism's role in Lessing's life is interesting. The survey of themes found in the African stories is useful before reading the collection, but less useful afterwards. Children of Violence differs from other serial novels because of its African subject matter, its "critical relation to the question of the position of women" (Thorpe dislikes "bigoted feminists"), and its inclusion of political material without simultaneously reducing characters to puppets. Concludes that Lessing should be spoken of in the company of Eliot, Hardy, Conrad and Lawrence.

252. Steele, M. C. "Children of Violence and Rhodesia:
A Study of Doris Lessing as Historical Observer."
The Central Africa Historical Association, 1974.
Local Series Pamphlet #29. Published by the
University of Rhodesia, Department of History,
P. O. Box MP167, Mt. Pleasant, Salisbury, Rhodesia.

The first four volumes of this novel series draw
from historical events in Southern Rhodesia in
the thirties and forties; this paper attempts to
assess Lessing's credibility as an historical
observer of those events. The author, a
historian, provides a useful historircal context,
unavailable anywhere else, for understanding
Lessing's early novels. He concludes that Lessing
is less than totally accurate historically and
questions the validity of her portrayal of white
society. He faults Lessing with having "missed
most of the social and political implications of
these vital post-war years, especially the movement to reform African economic and social
conditions of the forties and fifties."
For a response to Steele, read Diane Gage's
"The Relevance of History," Doris Lessing
Newsletter, 2 (Winter 1978), 4-5.

253. Schlueter, Paul, ed. A Small Personal Voice:
Essays, Reviews, Interviews. New York: Alfred A.
Knopf, 1974.

A collection of Lessing's essays on her life
and her work, on other writers, and on Africa.
It is an invaluable collection. The selctions
are the most significant of Lessing's essays,
including her "Preface to The Golden Noteboook,"
three interviews, and her writing on Sufism.
This book represents the only single volume
where one can read Lessing's exposition of her
craft.

254. Pratt, Annis and L. S. Dembo, eds. <u>Doris Lessing:</u>
      <u>Critical Studies</u>. Madison: University of Wisconsin
      Press, 1974.

> A reprint of the Autumn 1973 special issue on
> Lessing by <u>Contemporary Literature</u>. The essays
> included are: Howe, Florence. "A Conversation
> with Doris Lessing;" Carey, John L. "Art and
> Reality in <u>The Golden Notebook</u>;" Hinz, Evelyn J.
> and John J. Teunissen. "The Pietà as Icon in
> <u>The Golden Notebook</u>;" Morgan, Ellen. "Alienation
> of the Woman Writer in <u>The Golden Notebook</u>;" Zak,
> Michele Wender. "<u>The Grass is Singing</u>: A Little
> Novel About the Emotions;" Barnouw, Dagmar.
> "Disorderly Company: From <u>The Golden Notebook</u>
> to <u>The Four-Gated City</u>;" Sukenick, Lynn.
> "Feeling and Reason in Doris Lessing's Fiction;"
> Kaplan, Sydney Janet. "The Limits of
> Consciousness in the Novels of Doris Lessing;"
> Bolling, Douglass. "Structure and Theme in
> <u>Briefing for a Descent into Hell</u>;" Hardin, Nancy
> Shields. "Doris Lessing and the Sufi Way;"
> Krouse, Agate, Nesaule. "A Doris Lessing
> Checklist."

255. Rose, Ellen Cronan. <u>The Tree Outside the Window:</u>
      <u>Doris Lessing's Children of Violence</u>. Hanover,
      New Hampshire: University Press of New England,
      1976. Published on demand by University Micro-
      films International, Ann Arbor, Michigan 48106.

> This little known book is one of the most
> sensitive studies on the <u>Children of Violence</u>
> series. Using Erik Erikson's theory of
> ego-development to define Lessing's bildungsroman,
> Rose stresses that both the individual's develop-
> ment and the interaction between the individual
> and society must be considered. Asserts that
> Martha fails to achieve a sense of basic trust
> due to her unhappy childhood relationship to her
> mother, and she becomes an oral personality,
> passive in her interactions with the world.
> Martha must be reborn and create her own identity.
> Her quest is unassisted by familial trust and
> security or by coherent social institutions. She
> creates herself in part by finding metaphors
> which define her self, such as the "great bell of
> space." The strength of this study is Rose's
> sensitivity to the metaphoric progression from
> "the shell" to "the tree outside the window."
> Its weakness is Rose's inability to accept the
> prophetic dimension of the Appendix to <u>The Four-</u>
> <u>Gated City</u>. She calls this part Lessing
> destroying the world "by fiat."

256. Singleton, Mary Ann. The City and the Veld: the Fiction of Doris Lessing. Lewisburg: Bucknell University Press, 1977.

Deals with the major novels from The Grass is Singing through Memoirs. SIngleton argues that Lessing believes in a unified consciousness which integrates the ego-consciousness with the unconscious. The veld represents the world of Nature, associated with the unconscious, intuition, direct experience, and mindless repetition, while the city represents the world of society, associated with ego-consciousness, logic, symbolism, discursive thought, and fragmentation. The unification of these elements, which is embodied in the unified self, is represented by the City in the Veld, first described in Martha Quest. Singleton's argument draws heavily on Jungian psychology, as well as on the imagery of alchemy, and the influence of Sufism. She clearly relates these elements to each novel; however, her analysis often is too schematic and is foisted upon the novels. Singleton describes the City in the Veld as a state of mind, whereas Lessing moves through political realities to more enlightened social structures. Singleton's argument distorts Lessing's delicate balance between rationalism and irrationalism. The discussion of Briefing using the alchemical elements of the novel is most helpful, however.

257. Thorpe, Michael. Doris Lessing's Africa. London: Evans Brothers Ltd., 1978.

Argues that Lessing is essentially an African writer: "It is possible that everything she has written since she left Africa, not only her African writing, is the voice of such an exile." The period covered is from 1950-1965, between The Grass is Singing and Landlocked, although a chapter on the later published The Four-Gated City is included. Places Lessing in the English Romantic tradition of Wordsworth and Hardy, and in the socially conscious tradition of Thomas Mann. No specific school of criticism is used in the analysis of the works, but the analysis is careful and substantive. Lessing as the isolate, the outsider, is the perspective most consistently offered. A useful comparison is made betwen the Martha: Thomas Stern relationship to that of Marlow: Kurtz in The Heart of Darkness.

258. Rubenstein, Roberta. The Novelistic Vision of Doris
     Lessing: Breaking the Forms of Consciousness.
     Urbana, Illinois: University of Illinois Press, 1979.

> Undoubtedly the most comprehensive and useful
> critical commentary on Lessing to date. A
> chronological approach to all of the novels
> through The Memoirs of a Survivor is provided
> as well as attention to the cyclic design in
> which certain themes and narrative designs are
> returned to again and again. "The common
> denominator in Lessing's fictional world is the
> mind: the mind discovering, interpreting, and
> ultimately shaping its own reality." Rubenstein
> is particularly good at pointing out that the
> coherence of all the novels is the evolution of
> this conscious mind. The central tension in
> Lessing's work is the contrast between linear,
> analytic rational thought and circular, mythic,
> nonrational, symbolic thought. Rubenstein uses
> Jungian, Sufi, and literary techniques in order
> to discuss Lessing's lifelong study of "abnormal
> consciousness." This book carefully notes
> Lessing's movement away from realism to the
> symbolic mode of romanticism. Finally, in the
> chapter on The Golden Notebook, Rubenstein
> successfully tackles the critical questions which
> many others have evaded--the relationship between
> Anna and Lessing, the relationship between
> fictional structure and meaning, the purpose of
> doubling, and the relationship between fiction
> and reality.

GENERAL CRITICISM

259. Sachs, Joseph. "The Short Stories of Gordimer, Lessing,
     and Bosman" Trek, 15 (November 1951), 15-16.

260. McDowell, Frederic, P. W. "The Devious Involutions
     of Human Character and Emotions: Reflections of Some
     Recent British Novels." Wisconsin Studies in
     Contemporary Literature, 4 (Autumn 1963), 346-350.

> Primarily a review of The Golden Notebook and
> other mid-twentieth century novels, this article
> suggests that the novel is not aesthetically
> pleasing. "Mrs. Lessing demonstrates that a
> writer's intellectual equipment is ultimately more
> important than his intellectually unsupported
> formal instincts." The author asserts that
> Lessing's "deeper experience" results in a deeper
> "aesthetic commitment" than "the formally
> sophisticated novelists."

261. Howe, Florence. "Doris Lessing's Free Women" The
Nation, 11 January, 1965, 34-37.

> Ostensibly a review of the first two novels of
> Children of Violence and of The Golden Notebook,
> this essay is suggestive and insightful (for its
> time) concerning thematic issues in all of
> Lessing's fiction. Claims that Lessing's
> heroines move through a sense of division and
> fragmentation to madness or death. Her women
> are either unsuccessful at dying or live in the
> purgatory of inevitable suffering within the
> impersonal male-female struggle. Lessing's
> salient quality is her ability to speak to our
> lives.

262. McDowell, Frederick P. W. "The Fiction of Doris
Lessing: An Interim View.' Arizona Quarterly,
21 (Winter 1965), 315-345.

> A long critical survey of Lessing's works
> through Landlocked. The analysis of
> Lessing's realism is good, but there is no
> overriding thread which connects the analyses.
> Useful section on criticism of the short
> stories.

263. Kauffman, Stanley. "Literature of the Early Sixties."
Wilson Library Bulletin, 39 (May 1965), 751-752.

264. Brewer, Joseph E. "The Anti-Hero in Contemporary
Literature." Iowa English Year-Book, 12 (Fall 1967),
55-60.

> A rather dated discussion of several works,
> including A Man and Two Women, put in the
> context of the anti-hero.

265. Burkom, Selma R. "Only Connect: Form and Content in the Works of Doris Lessing." Critique, 11 (1968), 51-68.

> Comparison between E. M. Forester's admonishment to reconciliate opposites and that of Lessing to unite the individual and the collective. Lessing finds Jungian psychoanalysis too highly individualized and Marxist politics too completely dependent on the collective. Burkom argues that The Golden Notebook demonstrates the failure to connect at all levels and so do many of the short stories. She claims that Lessing believes that right personal relationships and an integrated view of life are possible if opposites are reconciled. The short sotry "Dialogue" is used to exemplify this hypothesis. Read Ellen Cronan Rose's article, "Statlier Mansion: Humanism Forster, and Lessing, " Massachusetts Review, 17 (Spring 1976), 200-212 for comparison.

266. Miller, C. "Called Kaffir Lover in Rhodesia." Saturday Review, 23 March 1968, 45-46.

267. McDowell, Frederick P. W. "Recent British Fiction: Some Established Writers." Contemporary Literature, 11 (Summer 1970), 424-428.

268. McDowell, Margaret B. "Reflections on the New Feminism. The Midwest Quarterly, 12 (April 1971), 309-335.

> A somewhat dated article which is primarily a critique of Kate Millett's book Sexual Politics with an aside to The Golden Notebook.

269. Spacks, Patricia Meyer. "Free Women." The Hudson Review, 24 (Winter 1971-72), 559-573.

> An informed, intelligent comparison of "emancipated women" as reflected in the work of Lilliam Hellman, Anais Nin, Doris Lessing, and Colette. The Golden Notebook, The Four-Gated City, and Briefing are all discussed from the viewpoint that freedom is impossible for women, since it depends for women on her connection with the male for orgasm. Instead madness or at the very least, self-obsession becomes synonymous with freedom, since it provides the freedom for self-discovery. Spacks suggests that Colette's form of freedom—the capacity for reconciliation with what is—is available only through the imagination's ability to illuminate and transform reality.

270. Drabble, Margaret. "Doris Lessing: Cassandra in a
      World Under Siege." Ramparts, 10 (February 1972),
      50-54.

         A basic essay on the meaning of "prophetic" as
         applied to Lessing. Drabble states that Lessing
         is "one of the very few novelists who have
         refused to believe the world is too complicated to
         understand."

271. Richey, Clarence W. "Professor Watkins' 'Sleep of
      Necessity'" A Note on the Parallel Between Doris
      Lessing's Briefing for a Descent into Hell and the
      G. I. Gurdjieff-P. D. Ouspensky System of Esoteric
      Psychology." Notes on Contemporary Literature,
      2 (March 1972), 9-11.

         Lessing's concept of organic life as primarily
         "food for the Moon" and the idea of a person's
         possible "Waking from sleep" are two common
         beliefs between Ouspensky's exposition of
         Gurdjieff's psychological system, In Search of the
         Miraculous, and Lessing's Briefing.

272. Mutti, Giuliana. "Female Roles and the Function of
      Art in The Golden Notebook." Massachusetts Studies in
      English, 3 (Spring 1972), 78-83.

         Asserts that "Anna Wulf's personality is merely a
         collection of roles, fragments of some total
         experience which the novel never approaches as
         fiction, in the novella, 'Free Women.'" The
         distinctions between fiction and reality break
         down as the Mashopi Hotel story provides the
         reality behind Frontiers of War, which if
         read carefully "is an exposure of Anna Wulf's
         idealogical position as a bourgeois white female
         living in colonized Africa." Similarly, The
         Shadow of the Third is Anna's attempt to write off
         her problems. The fiction provides the historical
         record, but does not provide the record of the
         disintegration caused by Anna's multiple roles.

273. Graves, Nora Calhoun. "Doris Lessing's Two Antheaps."
      Notes on Contemporary Literature, 2 (May 1972), 6-8.

         The other antheap to which the author alludes
         is the man-made antheap of the gold mine which
         figures in the short story of the same title.
         Graves, however, does not make clear the
         relationship of the two antheaps.

274.   Mulkeen, Anne M.   "Twentieth-Century Realism: The
       'Grid' Structure of The Golden Notebook."   Studies
       in the Novel, 4 (Summer 1972), 262-275.

       Mulkeen believes that the world of Anna Wulf
       is a "crisscrossing of the multiplicity of
       viewpoints (Anna as colonical emigre, novelist
       in the midst of artistic creation, Marxist
       humanist, psychotherapeutic patient, woman
       searching for love) with a multiplicity of events
       and issues, near and far through a series of
       stages in time."   The result is a "sense of
       interdependence of people, events, art and
       thought," with a sense of personal/cosmic
       disintegration.

275.   McDowell, Frederic P. W.   "Time of Plenty: Recent
       British Novels."   Contemporary Literature,
       13 (Summer 1972), 387-389.

       A short review of Lessing, especially, The
       Four-Gated City in the context of recent
       novels.   A rather general piece.

276.   Marchino, Lois.   "The Search for Self in the Novels
       of Doris Lessing."   Studies in the Novel, 4
       (Summer 1972), 252-262.

       The Golden Notebook, The Four-Gated City,
       and Briefing are discussed from the thematic
       perspective of the search for self in a world
       of alienated heroines.   The old world of the
       hero/heroine allowed for meaning to emerge
       from the coordinating myths of the group, but
       such support is an anachronism today.   The
       discussion of the theme is useful, but it is
       a much-discussed perspective.

277. Pratt, Annis. "Women and Nature in Modern Fiction."
Contemporary Literature, 13 (Autumn 1972), 476-490.

An examination of novels by women written
between 1896 and 1927 which, nonetheless,
includes Children of Violence. Pratt questions
whether the attitudes towards nature differ in
male and female fiction. She concludes that
"communion with the authentic self, first
achieved by the heroine [of women authors] in
early naturistic epiphanies, becomes a touchstone by which she holds herself together in the
face of destructive roles proffered to her by
society." Nature offers solace and normalcy
in the midst of the unnatural pressures of
society. Thus, the ecstasy presented in sexual
and naturistic moments in Lessing's works,
which are moments of visionary naturism, "have
no precise parallel in male fiction."

278. Karl, Frederik R. "Doris Lessing in the Sixties: The
New Anatomy of Melancholy." Contempoary Literature,
13 (Winter 1972), 15-33.

Undoubtedly, this essay is seminal in Lessing
criticism. Karl claims that Lessing's "literature
of enclosure" is comparable to that of Kafka,
Pinter, and Beckett in that all deal with space
only as a volume to be enclosed in rooms.
Within this space the self descends into the hell
of anxiety folded into neurosis. The anxiety
concerns unhappy male-female relationships which
are self-destructive, impotent, and profane.
Unlike D. H. Lawrence, Lessing does not look to
nature for renewal and transcendence over the
infinite, variable, messy quality of life as it is
lived. The existential woman of Simone de
Beauvoir is absent in Lessing. Instead, only the
nightmare of repetition is described.

279. Lang, Frances. "Doris Lessing's Madness as Ideology."
Off Our Backs, December 1972, 10-11.

A thematic overview of The Golden Notebook,
Children of Violence, and Briefing which does
not offer too much for the Lessing reader.
Lang claims that Lessing "misconstrues" the
meaning of self-discovery in these novels and
extols feeling over reason. Compare Lynn
Suckenick, "Feeling and Reason in Doris Lessing's
Fiction." Contempoary Literature, 14 (Autumn
1973), 98-118.

280. Porter, Nancy M.   " Way of Looking at Doris Lessing."
      In Female Studies VI.   Ed., Nancy Hoffman, Cynthia Secor,
      Andrian Tinsley.   New York: Feminist Press,
      1972, 123-138.

> An accounting of Children of Violence from
> the perspective of "silenced history." Such
> history includes the history of women, of native
> Africans, of displaced persons during World War
> II. Porter argues that Lessing is concerned with
> personal biography and history as they intersect
> in social structure and political event. In an
> unstable society discontinuity with the past and
> the future prevails. By recording the histories
> of those dislocated in time and space, Lessing
> gives voice to the silenced. This essay is
> important to feminist and to Marxist critics.

281. Webb, Marilyn. "Becoming the Men We Wanted to Marry."
      The Village Voice, 4 January 1973, 1, 14-17, 19.

> A personal documentation of Webb's sense of the
> women's movement and the non-directive role
> played in it by Lessing. Webb praises Lessing's
> refusal to play "guru" to the movement and urges
> all feminists to model their behavior instead
> on Lessing's serious regard for her own creative
> energy.

282. Brooks, Ellen W.   "The Image of Women in Lessing's
      The Golden Notebook." Critique, 15 (1973), 101-110.

> Brooks documents the division in Anna Wulf between
> the biologically determined, non-personal elements
> and the intellectually chosen, personal aspects of
> personality. Anna becomes liberated by giving
> rein to both aspects of herself in her
> relationship with Saul Green and by recognizing
> her human bi-sexuality. Little new perspective
> is offered by this essay.

283. Pratt, Annis. "Archetypal Approaches to the New Feminist Criticism." Bucknell Review, 21 (Spring 1973), 3-15.

> An investigation and defense of archetypal feminist criticism, particularly that which uses the linear myth of tthe hero's quest and the vertical myth of the journey into the psyche, or myth of rebirth. A brief but brilliant description of The Four-Gated City's correlation with Northrop Frye's "mythos of romance" will be of interest to Lessing readers, as will Pratt's excerpt from de Beauvoir's Second Sex as it applies to The Golden Notebook's treatment of sexual rivalry as a vehicle for questioniing the nature of human conflict and freedom.

284. Sudrann, Jean. "Hearth to Horizon: Changing Concepts of the 'Domestic' Life of the Heroine." The Massachusetts Review, 14 (Spring 1973), 235-256.

> Claims that the liberated heroine of modern novels by women cannot retreat into sheltered domesticity, as did Jane Eyre. Increasingly such heroines focus on the relationship between the public and the private world. Good discussion of the city as a unifying symbol of both the public and private domain; of the restoration of the Coleridge house as coherent with the restoration of personal and public history; and of Lessing's attempts to reinvest language with meaning in both the public and private domain. The latter discussion is not found elsewhere and is worth seeking out.

285. Hendin, Josephine. "Doris Lessing: The Phoenix 'Midst Her Fires." Harper, 346 (June 1973), 83-86.

> A review which is useful to read because Hendin interviewed Lessing in December 1972 and wrote this review afterwards.

286. Hynes, Joseph. "The Construction of The Golden
      Notebook." Iowa Review, 4 (Summer 1973), 100-113.

      Fundamental reading of the aesthetics and
      structure of this novel which should precede
      any detailed thematic examination of it.
      Hynes answers the most basic questions--who
      is the author, who is the audience, what are
      the motives, what are the occasions, where
      are the places (overt or moral), and what
      are the results or effects of choices. The
      significance of doubling, of Anna's relation
      to Saul, of the golden notebook section, and
      of the unity of the book are analyzed. Hynes
      concludes that all of us are The Golden Notebook's
      unity: that culminating presentation of the
      "fixedly fluid which is the name and being of
      Anna."

287. Barnouw, Dagmar. "Disorderly Company: From
      The Golden Notebook to The Four-Gated City."
      Contemporary Literature 14 (Autumn 1973), 491-515.
      Reprinted in Doris Lessing: Critical Studies,
      ed. Annis Pratt and L. S. Dembo. Madison: University
      of Wisconsin, 1974, 74-98.

      Claims that the differences between the novels
      are "indicative of changes in Lessing's concept
      of the function and responsibility of the novel-
      ist." There is a different attitude towards the
      protagonist and towards male-female relationships
      in each novel. In the former, the dilemma of the
      intelligent woman who has been conditioned to
      depend upon the man for her sense of self is
      expressed. Lessing is protective of Anna in a way
      she is not of Martha Quest. In The Golden
      Notebook, Lessing "superimposes structures of
      order on chaos" -- the four notebooks, and the
      Anna-Ella projection, for example. In The Four-
      Gated City Lessing supports the concept of self-
      knowledge as process by her narrative style.
      Her new belief in mutual male-female relationships
      affirms the possibility of this process.

288. Bolling, Douglass. "Structure and Theme in Briefing
      for a Descent into Hell." Contemporary Literature, 14
      (Autumn 1973), 550-565. Reprinted in Doris Lessing:
      Critical Studies, ed. Annis Pratt and L. S. Dembo.
      Madison: University of Wisconsin, 1974, 133-148.

          Theme and structure are tightly joined because
          Lessing wishes us to know that the unconscious
          is "everything" and the "thin layer of ego-
          identity" is very little. Bolling recognizes
          that the novel is limited by its "underemphasis
          on character and overemphasis on image, dream-
          like encounter or allegory," but he warns us not
          to judge it within "narrow formalist boundaries."
          Major images such as the crystalline sphere, the
          ancient city, the "singing light" are explained
          in the context of Watkkins's "recovery of fatal
          normalcy."

289. Carey, John L. "Art and Reality in The Golden Notebook."
      Contemporary Literature, 14 (Autumn 1973), 437-457.
      Reprinted in Doris Lessing: Critical Studies,
      ed. Annis Pratt and L. S. Dembo. Madison: University
      of Wisconsin, 1974, 20-40.

          One of the finest available articles on the
          structure of this novel. Claims that the
          structure tries to illustrate the fusion of
          art and life: "Reality thus comes to be
          understood as a complex interplay of objective
          experience and the subjective ordering of that
          experiecne by the artist. Life and art are
          seen as a single unit impossible to split."
          Art does not impose form on chaos; it is
          neither all fact nor all fiction. It does
          not split reality into parts and attempt to name
          it. Lessing brings Anna to the recognition that
          it is possible to compose a novel which "does not
          twist reality in a preconceived pattern...."
          The artist's responsibility is to give form to the
          nature of reality by "letting the form organically
          grow from the whole of reality...."

290. Hardin, Nancy Shields. "Doris Lessing and the Sufi
      Way." Contemporary Literature, 14 (Autumn 1973), 565–
      582. Reprinted in Doris Lessing: Critical Studies,
      ed. Annis Pratt and L. S. Dembo. Madison: University
      of Wisconsin, 1974, 148–165.

         An excellent introduction to the influence of
         Sufism on Lessing. The Four-Gated City, Briefing,
         and short stories from the Jack Orkney collection
         are discussed. Sufism attempts to awaken the
         individual, free him from the bonds of the ego and
         the rational mind, and to increase his capacity
         for more highly evolved states of mind, such as
         E. S. P. Receptivity, timing, and husbanding the
         received energy are all critical. All of
         Lessing's work in the 1970's has been influenced
         by Sufism; this artical is requisite.

291. Heinz, Evelyn J. and John J. Teunissen. "The Pieta as
      Icon in The Golden Notebook." Contemporary Literature,
      14 (Autumn 1973), 457–471. Reprinted in Doris Lessing:
      Critical Studies, ed. Annis Pratt and L. S. Dembo.
      Madison: University of Wisconsin, 1974, 40–54.

         A good example of archetypal criticism, this
         essay analyses the climactic final encounter
         between Saul Green and Anna Wulf. Saul's
         remark that "we can't either of us ever go
         lower than that," along with Anna's cradling
         of Saul in her arms suggests the Madonna of
         Michelangelo's Pietà. "What is played out is
         the other side of the role of the Great Mother—
         the death-dealing, revengeful, castrating
         female." Anna does not want to acknowledge
         this other side of motherly love—either in a
         personal or a collective sense. However,
         Anna's facing of these irrational forces in
         her life is ultimately beneficial and healthy.

292. Kaplan, Sydney Janet. "The Limits of Consciousness
in the Novels of Doris Lessing." Contemporary
Literature, 14 (Autumn 1973), 536-550. Reprinted in
Doris Lessing: Critical Studies, ed. Annis Pratt and
L. S. Dembo. Madison: University of Wisconsin, 1974
119-133.

Claims that Lessing's more recent fiction is less
concerned with the individual's unconscious or with
feminine consciousness than with the collective
unconscious. In The Four-Gated City there is a
movement away from the concept of consciousness as
self-contained and defined by words to the concept of
consciousness as a shared receptiveness. Words are
described as catalysts for meaning. Kaplan
coined the phrase "universal consciousness",
a useful term to describe Lessing's recent focus,
which is beyond being simply masculine or feminine.

293. Morgan, Ellen. "Alienation of the Woman Writer in
The Golden Notebook." Contemporary Literature, 14
(Autumn 1973), 471-481. Reprinted in Doris Lessing:
Critical Studies, ed. Annis Pratt and L. S. Dembo.
Madison: University of Wisconsin, 1974, 54-64.

Argues that Lessing is alienated from her
authentic perceptions of sexual politics because
there was no social corroboration for her perceptions. Anna-Ella's interpretations of her
experiences often belittle, deny, or distort her
experiences and censor her spontanteous responses
to them. Morgan suggests that this type of alienation
all women experience until they solidify into groups.
The essay does seem to ignore thae ironic tone of the
novel, however.

294. Sukenick, Lynn. "Feeling and Reason in Doris Lessing's
      Fiction." Contemporary Literature, 14 (Autumn 1973),
      515-535. Reprinted in Doris Lessing: Critical Studies,
      ed. Annis Pratt and L. S. Dembo. Madison: University
      of Wisconsin, 1974, 98-119.

         Lessing is committed to "something larger than
         private consciousness," and has always had an
         aversion to writing the "feminine novel,"
         according to Sukenick. Lessing is committed to
         "larger social issues" and sees the rational
         personality as the last defense against the
         irrational and the apparent loss of self.
         Althouugh both Anna Wulf and Martha Quest regain
         a connection to their own emotions, in both cases
         their work is filtered through an inquiring brain.
         This essay should be read in conjunction with
         Michael Magie's (College English, 38, Feb. 1977,
         581-552), as Sukenick refutes him on the grounds
         that Lessing is anti-Romantic, even in her
         deliberate use of the irrational in her later work.

295. Zak, Michele W. "The Grass is Singing: A Little Novel
      About the Emotions." Contemporary Literature, 14 (Autumn
      1973), 481-490. Reprinted in Doris Lessing: Critical
      Studies, ed. Annis Pratt and L. S. Dembo. Madison:
      University of Wisconsin, 1974, 64-74.

         Suggests that this novel represents the dialectical
         relationship between the "individual circumstances
         of one's life and the material nature of the social
         and economic system within which one lives." It
         is both a "documentation of Mary Turner's
         psychological disintegration" as well as a "keen-edged
         analysis of the state and quality of women's lives
         in a colonial society."

296. Spencer, Sharon. "Femininity and the Woman Writer:
      Doris Lessing's The Golden Notebook and the Diary
      of Anais Nin." Women's Studies, 1, No. 3 (1973),
      347-359.

         Believes that the woman artist must accept the
         traditional male qualities (her animus) as well
         as her traditional female qualities (her anima)
         in order to create. In each of these works the
         author explores the painful process of accepting
         her animus. The discussion of The Golden Notebook
         focuses on Anna's dream of the deformed spiteful
         old person and on her sense that Saul Green is
         her symbolic twin. Compare this essay to Ellen
         Morgan's piece (Contemporary Literature, 14, Autumn
         1973, 471-481.)

297. O'Fallon, Kathleen. "Quest for a New Vision." World
Literature Written in English, 12 (November 1973), 180-189.

An archetypal approach to The Golden Notebook and
The Four-Gated City, this essay uses the archetype of
the hero's descent to the underworld, the battle with
a monster, and the rebirth into society with a new
knowledge of the self. Not much fresh insight,
however.

298. Porter, Nancy. "Silenced History—Children of Violence and
The Golden Notebook." World Literature Written in English,
12 (November 1973), 161-179.

A very similar essay to the Female Studies VI (see
#280) essay by Porter, except this one includes
material on The Golden Notebook. The discussion
of Anna's psychological time (the time of the
notebooks) and her conventional story-telling
time (in Free Women) is illuminating.

299. Pratt, Annis. "The Contrary Structure of Doris Lessing's
The Golden Notebook." World Literature Written in English,
12 (November 1973), 150-161.

Stresses the similarities between Anna Wulf's
contrary states of mind and William Blake's
description of "contraries." Anna's contraries
are openness to experience, albeit chaotic experience vs. cynicism and rigidity to experience.
Even the structure of the novel depends on contrary
responses to specific experiences. Pratt also
discusses Lessing's insistence on androgyny or
integrated sexuality for the integrated self, a
concept shared by both Jung and Blake.

300. Seligman, Dee. "The Sufi Quest." World Literature Written
in English, 12 (November 1973), 190-206.

Claims that Landlocked and The Four-Gated City are
part of a sequence which can best be understood
through the context of Sufi ideas. Martha journies
inward to locate her Sufi self. Sufism is explained
and Thomas Stern is described as Martha's Sufi
teacher. Martha Quest moves through four stages of
individual evolution towards a higher consciousness
in The Four-Gated City. The Appendix of this novel
seems integrated with the rest of the novel if it
is read from the perspective of its Sufi content.

301. Sanderson, Annette. "The Fragmented Heroine." The Harvard
Advocate, 106 (Winter 1973), 65-67.

A brief summary of two novels by Joan Didion,
Slouching Towards Bethlehem and Play It as It Lays
and two by Lessing, The Golden Notebook and
The Four-Gated City. Little new insight is shed.

302. Porter, Dennis. "Realism and Failure in The Golden
Notebook." Modern Language Quarterly, 35 (March 1974),
56-65.

Claims that realism is a tool used against itself by
Lessing. The most important art for her is that which
expresses the grim truth of life "without neutralizing
it in a conventional narrative or transcending it by
the creative imagination." Lessing finds realism
unable to tell "the truth;" it is an art of
"approximation and ironic accomodation and not of
truth." We must experience Anna Wulf's dissatis-
faction with this form and recognize the purpose for
which Lessing employs realism in the novel.

303. Aycock, Linnea. "The Mother-Dauther Relationship in the
Children of Violence Series." Anonymous: A Journal for
the Woman Writer, 1 (Spring 1974), 48-56. (Published
by Women's Studies Program, California State University,
Fresno.)

Jung's analysis of the mother-complex is used to
discuss Martha Quest's relationship to her mother.
Jung provides a more positive point of view about
the mother-daughter conflict than is generally
suggested: those daughters who fight through
their resistance to their mothers gain a new sort
of self-knowledge. This idea makes clear the
relationship between Martha's discovery of the
self-hater and her mother's visit to her in
London.

304. Lewis, M. Susan. "Conscious Evolution in The Four-Gated
     City." Anonymous: A Journal for the Woman Writer,
     1 (Spring 1974), 56-71. (Published by Women's Studies
     Program, California State University, Fresno.)

     The Sufi concept of conscious evolution is applied
     to Martha's learning four laws of nature in each
     of the four sections of the novel. She learns the
     law of inevitable choice, that is, there is free
     will to choose among pre-determined alternatives;
     she learns that the nature of learning is a
     recognition of something that one had already
     known; she learns that she is part of a cycle and
     her experiences are impersonal, universal; she
     witnesses an increased need for evolution or more
     complete understanding. Both the Coleridge children
     and the mutant children of the Appendix have this
     collective knowledge and capacities of humankind.

305. Silva, Nancy Neufield. "Doris Lessing's Ideal Reconcilia-
     tion." Anonymous: A Journal for the Woman Writer, 1
     (Spring 1974), 72-81. (Published by Women's Studies
     Program, California State University, Fresno.)

     Using Burkom's idea that Lessing wishes to
     .reconcile antitheses and make connections in order
     to see life wholly, the author examines "A Sunrise on
     the Veld," "The Eye of God in Paradise", and
     "Dialogue". The use of Burkom's idea is
     simplistic but there is a good discussion of Jung's
     concept of "the shadow" in connection with these
     stories. A useful essay for those teaching the
     short stories.

306. Tiger, Virginia. "Advertisements for Herself." The
     Columbia Forum, 3 (Spring 1974), 15-20.

     A discussion of The Golden Notebook and The
     Summer Before the Dark as women's confessional
     novels. Autobiographical and fictional impulses
     converge in this area of literature. Hallmarks
     of this mode are the submergence in self, the
     sense of limited engagement with life, the
     first-person point of view, the crisis in
     function, the passion for the enclosed space,
     the birth of a new, authentic self, and the use
     of the female friend as doppelgänger.

307. West, Rebecca. "And they All Lived Unhappily Ever After." Times Literary Supplement, 3777 (26 July 1974), 779.

Doris Lessing's works are put into the context of contemporary wmen's fiction, including the work of Margaret Drabble, Iris Murdoch and Edna O'Brien. Lessing is described as the "English George Sand," ...a formidable woman, who can carry with her such a heavy intellectual satchel..." and who "plainly cannot believe that women can hope for satisfactory sex lives."

308. Libby, Marion Vlastos. "Sex and the New Woman in The Golden Notebook." Iowa Review, 5 (Fall 1974), 106-120.

Contends that The Golden Notebook is not a feminist novel because Lessing fails to affirm the key tenets of contemporary feminist philosophy. Lessing does not place the blame on men often enough; men are allowed to be less committed to women than vice-versa; men do not experience the same physiologic closeness to children and to their sensuality that women do; female sexuality is portrayed as "positive submissiveness." The article assumes a congruity between Anna Wulf and Lessing, an assumption which should be clarified.

309. Joyner, Nancy. "The Underside of the Butterfly: Lessing's Debt to Woolf." The Journal of Narrative Technique, 4 (September 1974), 204-212.

Using To the Lighthouse and The Golden Notebook, Joyner compares and contrasts Woolf and Lessing in a manner useful for classroom purposes. Although there are obvious stylistic and organizational differences, both writers "distort time and alternate point of view" to achieve their ends. Lily Briscoe is more liberated than Anna Wulf because she is not dependent on male approval, but both feel the need to "build up" the male ego. Woolf's novel ends optimistically, whereas Lessing's ending is ambiguous.

310. Craig, Joanne. "The Golden Notebook: The Novelist as Heroine." University of Windsor Review, 10 (Fall-Winter 1974), 55-66.

An attempt to define the structure of the novel. Craig concludes that the book is "a sort of model" of the mind itself, in the way that "images, events, characters arise from its superficial formlessness and link up horizontally and vertically, across temporal and topical categories...." The essay is not very precise.

311. Brown, Lloyd, W. "The Shape of Things: Sexual Images and
      the Sense of Form in Doris Lessing's Fiction." World
      Literature Written in English, 14 (April 1975), 176-187.

          An interesting discussion of Lessing's interest
          in the mannequin image and its relation to her
          suspicion of established patterns or forms.
          Argues that Lessing integrates "the design of each
          novel (A Proper Marriage, The Golden Noteboook, and
          The Summer Before the Dark) with those very images
          and forms through which she has demonstrated the
          essentially suspect nature of formal designs.

312. Rubenstein, Roberta. "Doris Lessing's The Golden Notebook:
      The Meaning of Its Shape." American Imago, 32 (Spring
      1975), 40-58.

          Argues that fiction and fact are deliberately mingled,
          that Saul Green is a projection of negative parts of
          Anna's self as well as of her positive sources of
          creative energy, and that "truth" is measured by no
          one version of experience but by all the versions
          seen together. Usefully read with John Carey's
          essay (#289) as well as those by Hynes (#286),
          Lifson (#356), and Seligman (#1012).

313. Rubenstein, Roberta. "Outer Space, Inner Space: Doris
      Lessing's Metaphor of Science Fiction." World Literature
      Written in English, 14 (April 1975), 187-198.

          This essay defines the way most critics now read
          Lessing's later fiction. "Her 'space fiction'
          is not about outer space at all but about inner
          space. It is more accurately, a metaphor
          through which she portrays her imagined-but
          utterly realistic--extension of the present, to
          show us the human and emotional contexts through
          which the future might be met and redirected.
          The solution is ... the intelligent use of our
          own psychic and emotional resources. The Four-
          Gated City and Briefing are the examples."

314. Spilka, Mark. "Lessing and Lawrence: The Battle of the Sexes." Contemporary Literature, 16 (Spring 1975), 218-240.

A seminal article on Lessing which provides not only a comparison to Lawrence but also sugests a critical context for Lessing in the romatic movement. The novels considered are The Golden Notebook, Women in Love, The Rainbow, and Lady Chatterly's Lover.

Structurally Lessing's work differs from Lawrence's. However, like Lawrence, Lessing believes that the philosophical novel can help to create wholeness. Like Lawrence, Lessing is modern in her sensibility but traditional in her desires for naturalism. Both authors draw on landscape and animal life for images which serve as a foil to the image of the unreal, self-absorbed urban existence. Spilka claims that Lessing shares and "modifies" Lawrence's premises concerning "real men" and sensual power rather than refutes him. Both novelists in middle age move beyond sexuality to a new selfhood.

315. Stein, Karen F. "Reflections in a Jagged Mirror: Some Metaphors of Madness." Aphra, 6 (Spring 1975), 2-11.

The image of the mirror as the reflection of the socially fabricated self and its concommitant symbolic association with the imagination and consciousness is the focus. The Summer Before the Dark and The Four-Gated City provide "more constructive resolution of their dilemmas" than do Sylvia Plath or Charlotte Perkins Gilman's works, which are also discussed.

316. Lightfoot, Marjorie J. "Breakthrough in The Golden Notebook." Studies in the Novel, 7 (Summer 1975), 277-285.

"In The Golden Notebook, Doris Lessing shows the effect on individuals of the chaotic experience of twentieth century political and social upheaval... the author actually attempts to 'break a form' and 'break certain forms of consciousness to go beyond them...Mrs. Lessing does more than reveal the blurred line betwen 'facts' and 'fiction' in the novel: by breaking through form to reflect content, she demonstrates the capacity of the individual to break out of repeated patterns of failure." (M.J.L.)

317. Ryf, Robert S. "Beyond Ideology: Doris Lessing's Mature
      Vision." Modern Fiction Studies, 21 (Summer 1975),
      193-201.

           Claims that Briefing connects to Lessing's earlier
           novels in its "movement beyond ideology, which takes
           shape in the emerging opposition to and final
           rejection of categories, and the recognition of the
           primacy of experiential insights and values as
           against abstract knowledge and norms." Like
           The Golden Notebook and The Four-Gated City, Briefing
           emphasizes the inadequacy of language and of logic.
           Ryf argues that Lessing uses mental breakdown as the
           self's attempt to escape categories which merely trap
           and fragment the self. Claims that the novel's end
           is not pessimistic.

318. Clements, Frances M. "Lessing's 'One Off the Short List'
      and the Definition of Self." Frontiers, 1 (Fall 1975),
      106-109.

           An analysis of the short story which focuses on
           the reversal of traditional male and female use of
           sexuality to prove self-worth.

319. Lefcowitz, Barbara. "Dreams and Action in Lessing's
      The Summer Before the Dark." Critique: Studies in
      Modern Fiction, 17 (December 1975), 107-119.

           A clarification of the seal symbol in this novel.
           The seal is an analogue for the self but the
           false self demanded by a patriachal society which
           burdens women. Kate must abandon the seal image
           in order to free herself of the illusion that her
           self is embodied by something helpless and lowly.
           Lefcowitz concludes that at the end Kate's
           imaginative life is more expansive than the
           realistic possibilities of the life in Blackheath
           to which she returns.

320. Ahearn, Marie. "Science Fiction in the Mainstream Novel:
      Doris Lessing." In Proceedings of the Fifth National
      Convention of the Popular Culture Association, ed. Michael
      T. Marsden (Bowling Green: Bowling Green State University,
      Popular Press, 1975), 1277-1296.

           Primarily a summary of Briefing, this paper offers
           little new perspective. However, the author does
           suggest a positive reading for the section concerning
           the convening of the gods, a much maligned portion
           of the novel.

321. Ferrier, Carole. "Lives in Conflict: Doris Lessing's
     Children of Violence Novels." Hecate, 1 (February 1975).
     31-45.

        Basically an overview of the major themes within
        the novel series, this essay does deal with reader
        response to Lessing's apparent disinterest in
        political activism. Martha's exploration of her own
        psyche in The Four-Gated City becomes "almost a
        history of the development of psychological theory
        and research from Freud to recent anti-psychiatry
        and parapsychology." The essay reflects the
        changing critical receptiveness to Lessing's
        ideas.

322. Markow, Alice Bradley. "The Pathology of Feminine Failure
     in the Fiction of Doris Lessing." Critique: Studies in
     Modern Fiction, 16, No. 1 (1975), 88-100.

        Rather basic treatment of Lessing's women being
        failures in the traditional roles of mother and
        wife and representing the new professional woman.
        Markow surveys The Grass is Singing, The Golden
        Notebook, The Four-Gated City, and The Summer Before
        the Dark and concludes that Lessing believes "woman
        will have to surmout her nostalgia for the
        dependent life...she will have to extirpate her
        need for romantic love...she will have to assume
        responsibility for a self."

323. Olsen, F. Bruce. "A Sunrise on the Veld: An Analysis."
     In Insight II: Analyses of Modern British Literature,
     ed. J. V. Hagopian and M. Dolch. Frankfurt Am Main:
     Hirschgraben-Verlag, 1975, 234-238.

        A clear analysis of the distance between persona
        and the interior monologue in this short story.
        This analysis is very useful because the technique
        of establishing distance between persona and author
        is used by Lessing in her Children of Violence
        series as a literary vehicle for evaluating the
        novel's content.

324. Rapping, Elayne Antler. "Unfree Women: Feminism in Doris Lessing's Novels." Women's Studies, 3, No. 1 (1975), 29-44.

Cogently traces Lessing's movement away from individualism and feminism and towards a collective feminine consciousness which transcends personalities and individual ideas. The Golden Notebook exemplifies the former and The Four-Gated City the latter. There is an excellent analysis of Lessing's technique of filtering public events through the "veil of feminine sensibility, producing a multi-dimensional vision, or perhaps revision of history, in which women emerge as collective heroines, molding, preserving, and interpreting the forms of life which make history possible." Martha as housekeeper suggests the world of all female experience, trapped in the home, and finding her inner space as psychic freedom.

325. Rose, Ellen Cronan. "The Eriksonian Bildungsroman: An Approach Through Doris Lessing." Hartford Studies in Literature, 7, No. 1 (1975), 1-17.

An application of Eriksonian ego-psychology to the bildungsroman. This type of psychoanalysis incorporates the dialectic between the individual's psycho-dynamics and his environment. Although the focus of this article is on critical theory rather than on Lessing's work, the discussion of Martha Quest's failure to acquire "basic trust" and her consequent orality is fascinating. Much of this material is incorporated into Rose's book The Tree Outside the Window (Hanover, N. H.: University Press of New England, 1976). Gohlman's article (South Atlantic Bulletin, 43, November 1978, 95-107) should be read after this one.

326. Rose, Ellen Cronan. "Statlier Mansions: Humanism,
      Forster, and Lessing." The Massachusetts Review,
      17 (Spring 1976), 200-212.

          A comparison between E. M. Forster's humanism
          in Howard's End and Doris Lessing's in The Four-
          Gated City. The humanistic belief in a
          correspondence between the individual and his
          social values as a measure of reality is a
          faith shared by both writers. However, Lessing's
          humanism is a modified version of Forster's.
          The Coldridge house in Bloomsbury and Mary Butts'
          cottage both suggest models of connection and
          sanity, but neither can withstand the pressures
          of modern reality. The exterior world is a
          reflection of the chaos and fragmentation of
          the individual psyche. Only new existential
          categories, new houses, and new structures can
          express new psychological realities. Lessing
          may yet fulfill the old humanist ideal of
          creating congruences, although in new forms.

327. Rubenstein, Roberta. "Briefing on Inner Space:
      Doris Lessing and R. D. Laing." Psychoanalytic
      Review, 63 (Spring 1976), 83-95.

          Explores specific paralles between Charles
          Watkin's experience in Briefing and those
          of Jesse Watkins in Laing's The Politics
          of Experience. Rubenstein concludes that
          Lessing, unlike Laing, does not fully
          trust the schizophrenic's experience as a
          healing response to our current madness.
          The mystic truth which Charles Watkins
          rediscovers involves guilt and destruction
          as well as innocence and harmony.

328. Vlastos, Marion. "Doris Lessing and R. D. Laing:
      Psychopolitics and Prophecy." PMLA, 91 (March
      1976), 245-257.

      The Golden Notebook, The Four-Gated City, and
      Briefing are all analyzed in Laingian terms.
      Both Laing and Lessing see the mad person as
      a "symptom and victim of a sick society" and
      "as prophet of a possible new world, a
      world governed by forces of unity rather than
      separation." The ideological treatment of
      madness in the first two novels seems consistent
      and the ideas are expanded in Briefing. Vlastos
      argues that Lessing is fatalistic in believing
      that there is an inherent duality which requires
      a simultaneous existence in both worlds that
      is difficult to maintain. What is most
      important to Lessing is the immutable nonhuman
      world of the divine.

329. Carnes, Valerie. "Chaos, That's the Point: Art as
      Metaphor in Doris Lesisng's The Golden Notebook."
      World Literature Written in English, 15 (April 1976),
      17-28.

      Suggests that the circular structure of the novel
      allows Anna to "create" her own life just as she
      once had "created" her daughter's day with bed-
      time sstories. Too much plot summary to be
      of much interest to serious readers.

330. Spacks, Patricia Meyer. "Only Personal: Some Function
      of Fiction." The Yale Review, 65 (June 1976), 528-544.

      Discusses the relative value of fiction and
      fact when human life lacks coherence. Part of
      Lessing's purpose in The Golden Notebook is to
      establish the importance of the form used to
      render experience. Anna attempts to accept the
      pain of life, while Phillip Roth's characters,
      especially Tarnopol of My Life as a Man, attempts
      to turn his life into fiction in order to avoid
      the pain of reality. Lessing's persona is
      conscious of the world, while Roth's persona is
      a narcissist who knows only the personal order
      he creates.

331. Rose, Ellen Cronan. "A Briefing for Briefing:
Charles Williams' Descent into Hell and Doris
Lessing's Briefing for a Descent into Hell."
Mythlore, 4 (September 1976), 10-15.

> Claims that Williams' novel provides a
> "referential context for defining the form or
> genre of Lessing's strange book" and that "it
> anatomizes the thematic conerns which are
> embedded in Lessing's narrative." "...It
> suggests a way of defining Lessing's relation to
> the Romantic tradition to which Charles Williams
> belongs." Lessing's book is a "romance with an
> anti-romance" because it exhibits typically
> Romantic statements on the nature of reality but
> lacks the Romantic faith in correspondences
> between ideas and things. A useful essay for
> comparison is Michael Magie's "Doris Lessing
> and Romanticism" (College English, 38, February
> 1977, 531-552.)

332. Krouse, Agate Nesaule. "Doris Lessing's Feminist
Plays." World Literature Written in English, 15
(November 1976), 305-322.

> A useful exegesis of Play with a Tiger and
> Each His Own Wilderness. The former play
> suggests some important contrasts to The
> Golden Notebook, such as, the fact that the
> play is exclusively about the sex war. Each His Own
> Wilderness is the stronger dramatic work and raises
> feminist questions concerning maternal
> responsibility to children.

333. Bolling, Douglass. "Thoughts on Jack Orkney."
Doris Lessing Newsletter, 1 (Winter 1976), 1, 8, 9.

> The source of Jack Orkney's strength as a
> novella is described as a "balancing of rhythms,
> claims, tensions." In particular, the
> balancing of the needs of the ego and of the
> unconscious is stressed. Bolling's ideas are
> fecund.

334. Marquit, Doris G. "A Note on Martha Quest's 'Inspiration'
by Lenin." Doris Lessing Newsletter, 1 (Winter 1976), 6.

> An explication of an allusion in A Ripple
> from the Storm to a quotation attributed to
> Lenin but actually written by another Russian
> author.

335. Rose, Ellen Cronan. "The End of the Game: New Directions in Doris Lessing's Fiction." The Journal of Narrative Technique, 6 (Winter 1976), 66-75.

   Claims that Lessing has turned to writing "metafiction" since The Golden Notebook. Using Ella's novel in this book as her paradigm, Rose explores Lessing's new found Jungian sense of reality. If the novel is to embody truthfully the nature of reality it must include both the disorder of surface reality, of the world of the ego, and the order of the deeper reality, or the world of the collective unconscious. Lessing's literary technique has become a surface story and an underlying motif. Ultimately, the reader must abandon the traditional rational concept of reality and embrace the irrational experiences as well as the rational ones.

336. Sprague, Claire. "Olive Schreiner: Touchstone for Lessing." Doris Lessing Newsletter, 1 (Winter 1976), 4-5, 9-10.

   A comparative study of Lessing's reading of Schreiner's The Story of an African Farm with Dan Jacobson's reading of the novel. Lessing "circumscribes pessimism" in a way that Schreiner did not, according to Sprague. "Lessing needs the whole of Schreiner as a touchstone, as another self she needs to understand, emulate, and finally to escape. Dan Jacobson finds Schreiner's artist self her most usable self."

337. Soos, Emese. "Revolution in the Historical Fiction of Jean-Paul Sartre and Doris Lessing." Perspectives on Contemporary Literature (Publication of the Conference on Twentieth Century Literature), 2, No. 1 (1976), 23-33.

   Sartre and Lessing have each written novel cycles which presumed the historical success of the Communist Party. However, the Communist revolution at least temporarily failed, and each writer had the need to account for historical circumstance before the completion of their cycles. Lessing, Soos claims, "abandoned her faith that political activism could effectuate lasting change" after her disillusionment with the Party. Instead, she shows her partisans' motives as suspect (e. g., Anton Hesse's motives) and depicts the vagaries of the East-West political alliances. She turns to "mystical consciousness" because of her disillusionment.

338. Magie, Michael L. "Doris Lessing and Romanticism."
     College English, 38 (February 1977), 531-552.

> An extremely important essay which clearly
> critiques Lessing's philosophical position.
> Argues that Lessing's Romantic mode, i.e., her
> rejection of the Rationalist tradition, is the
> inherent decadent weakness of her work. Magie
> uses _The Golden Notebook_, _The Four-Gated City_,
> _Briefing_, and _Memoirs_ to substantiate his
> point that Lessing's belief in irrationalism,
> in the mad as more highly evolved human specimens,
> in the impossibility of having a self, in the
> artist as prophet, and in knowledge as a fiction is
> mere folly. He argues not only that this idea of
> mind has been competently refuted by philosophers
> but also, and more importantly, that Lessing offers
> counter examples within her own works to Romantic
> ontology. He asserts that Lessing is in conflict
> between irrationalism and her own truthful,
> rational, and generous art which is in real sympathy
> for the living experiences of other human beings.
> Lessing uses the Aristotlean tools of definition
> and controlled predication in order to convey an
> essentially mystical vision. The response to this
> article which should be read is Judith Stitzel's
> "Reading Doris Lessing" (_College English_, 40,
> January 1979, 498-505.)

339. Eder. Doris L. "Briefings for a Descent into Hell:
     The Writer's Consciousness Confronts Apocalypse." _Modern
     British Literature_, 2 (Spring 1977), 98-116.

> A rambling, disconnected article with many points
> familiar to Lessing scholars. _The Golden Notebook_,
> _The Four-Gated City_, and _Briefing_ are cited to show
> that the artist is representative of the twentieth
> century consciousness. Eder argues that Lessing is
> a "cosmicist" and not a humanist. The evolution of
> consciousness and the simultaneous attraction to and
> repulsion from dissolution is a unifying theme of
> these novels.

340. Hardin, Nancy Shields. "The Sufi Teaching Story and Doris
      Lessing." Twentieth Century Literature, 23 (October 1977),
      314-325.

> Argues that "Out of the Fountain," The Summer Before
> the Dark, and Memoirs all make use of such character-
> istic components of Sufi teaching stories as an
> openended setting and characters, dreams as fables
> or sources of information, repetition of an ex-
> perience to recall what is forgotten and a sense
> of the world "transmuted, and in another key."
> "Drawing materials from the actual world on the one
> hand and from the mental processes on the other,
> Lessing suggests the possibilities of a single,
> whole experience. The secret is one of assimilation;
> for Lessing, as the Sufis, does not see the two as
> separate."

341. LeBeau, Cecilia H. "The World Behind the Wall." Doris
      Lessing Newsletter, 1 (Fall, 1977), 7, 10.

> A comparison of Eugene Zamiatin's novel, We,
> with Memoirs. Both works use the figure of
> two worlds separated by a figurative and literal
> wall.

342. Lightfoot, Marjorie J. "'Fiction' vs. 'Reality': Clues
      and Conclusions in The Golden Notebook." Modern British
      Literature, 2 (Fall 1977), 182-188.

> Important, though brief, piece on the form of the
> novel and its relation to Anna's quest for in-
> tegration. Argues that the Anna of Free Women
> is defeated and settles for the "second rate"
> dryly and ironically, but that the Anna who
> writes The Golden Notebook is successfully in-
> tegrated. This "real" Anna abandons the four
> notebooks, writes "the golden notebook," breaks
> out of narcissism in the dream of essential
> human courage, gives the golden notebook to
> Saul, and acknowledges the negative consequences
> of self-division by writing of them in Free Women.
> This essay attacks directly the central question
> of the ending of the novel.

343. Stitzel, Judith. "The Uses of Humor." Doris Lessing
     Newsletter, 1 (Fall 1977), 2-3.

     Focuses on a little discussed element of Lessing's
     work--humor. Claims that "evasion of the truth
     about others and about oneself are inextricably
     bound for Lessing. Both are possible through
     humor, and both are dangerous." A fuller treat-
     ment of this subject is Stitzel's "Humor and
     Survival in the Works of Doris Lessing,"
     Regionalism and the Female Imagination, 4 (Fall
     1978), 61-68.

344. Gerver, Elisabeth. "Women Revolutionaries in the Novels
     of Nadine Gordimer and Doris Lessing." World Literature
     Written in English, 17 (April 1978), 38-50.

     An interesting attempt to discuss Children of
     Violence in terms of Lukacs' notion of critical
     realism, in which the individual and the society
     are intertwined, as well as private interests
     and public affairs. Turgenev and Conrad's
     revolutionary women are compared to those of
     Gordimer and Lessing. Though brief, this essay
     contains one of the few useful discussions of
     A Ripple from the Storm.

345. Chaffee, Patricia. "Spatial Patterns and Closed Groups
     in Lessing's African Stories." South Atlantic Bullentin,
     43 (May 1978), 42-52.

     One of the few articles concerning Lessing's
     African material. Claims that conflicts between
     "insiders" and "outsiders," be they white vs.
     black, adult vs. child, men vs. women, or
     Afrikaaners vs. English, are expressed in terms of
     physical and psychological boundaries, that is,
     outer space and inner space. Particularly in-
     teresting is the discussion of male vs. female
     response to the open African landscape.

346. Thorpe, Michael. "The Grass is Singing." In The Literary
     Half-Yearly. Ed. Anniah Gowda. Vol. 19 (July 1978), 17-
     27.

     A reasonable analysis of the novel's central themes,
     this essay addresses such questions as the vague,
     shadowy portrayal of Moses. Thorpe also discusses
     the relationship of the novel's title to Eliot's
     The Wasteland.

347. Fishburn, Katherine. "Anti-American Regionalism in the
      Fiction of Doris Lessing." Regionalism and the Female
      Imagination, 4 (Fall 1978), 19-25.

      Lessing's anti-American statements and implications
      from them are drawn largely from The Golden
      Notebook, The Four-Gated City, and The Summer Before
      the Dark. Since Lessing believes that the world is
      a single organism, she views the overweening power
      of one nation, the United States, a society full of
      neuroses, aggression, and dissatisfied men and women,
      as a threat to all. The point made is rather small,
      although not discussed elsewhere.

348. Stitzel, Judith. "Humor and Survival in the Works of Doris
      Lessing." Regionalism and the Female Imagination, 4 (Fall
      1978), 61-68.

      An excellent discussion of an overlooked quality
      of Lessing's works--humor. Lessing does not
      emphasize laughter as a healthy, humanizing
      activity. Instead, laughter may derive from self-
      mockery and self-rejection, as in Matty's clowning.
      Or it may be contrived laughter, used to numb
      oneself from what is painful. Another form of
      laughter is cynicism, which is particularly
      destructive since it takes away the energy for
      change. A creative form of laughter is found in
      the Nasrudin jokes of Sufi literature, which Lessing
      makes use of. Inherent in the joke's methodology is
      the ability to see something in a new way, breaking
      through conditioned responses. Giggling, the
      laughter of the mad at the disporportions of the world,
      is also heard in Lessing. Most often what is heard
      in her works is the sound of derision.

349. Gohlman, Susan A. "Martha Hesse of The Four-Gated City:
      A Bildungsroman Already Behind Her." South Atlantic
      Bulleting, 43 (November 1978), 95-107.

      Claims that in each of the four parts of this
      novel Martha is forming a new identity, after
      rejecting that old burlesque of herself, "Matty".
      In the first section, Martha "discovers the
      relationship between Matty and 'Martha the
      Defender.'" In the second part, through her
      "memory work" Martha understands the cliché of
      possessive mother and rebellious daughter. In
      the third part, Martha recognizes the source
      of energy is outside herself. In the fourth part,
      Martha recognizes that her own development of the
      self-hater, "Matty," was her own survival mechanism
      which Lynda Coldridge lacked. She discovers the
      underlying unity of those opposed emotions which
      have in the past controlled her.

350. Brown, Ruth Christiani. "Martha's Quest: An Echo of Psyche's." Doris Lessing Newsletter, 2 (Winter 1978), 8-10.

> Claims that echoes of the Amor and Psyche myth underlie all of the Children of Violence series. "The myth provides a unifying design for Lessing's compelling picture of Martha's search for self..." Psyche's four labors demanded by Aphrodite parallel Martha's actions and her "emregence into individuality provides the prototype for Martha's escape from traditional roles and her development of selfhood."

351. Lukens, Rebecca. "Inevitable Ambivalence: Mother and Daughter in Doris Lessing's Martha Quest." Doris Lessing Newsletter, 2 (Winter 1978), 13-14.

> Believes that Martha Quest " has at its center Martha's complex conflicts, her self-examination, and her comparisons between the realities of her mother's life and Martha's expectations for her own." This essay might be useful for those teaching the novel.

352. Marchino, Lois. "Life, Lessing, and the Pursuit of Feminist Criticism." Doris Lessing Newsletter, 2 (Winter 1978), 1, 15-16.

> This essay suggests that Lessing is a feminist, despite her protestations to the contrary. However, since Lessing assumes that other areas with which she is concerned don't fit into that rubric, she refuses the rubric. "The resolution is the realization of feminism as all-encompassing."

353. Matsue, Harve. "A Personal Observation on "The Sun Between Their Feet.'" Doris Lessing Newsletter, 2 (Winter 1978), 11.

> A brief essay which presents a Japanese undergraduate's response to the philosophical issues of the story.

354. Sarvan, Charles and Liebetraut. "D. H. Lawrence and Doris
Lessing's The Grass is Singing." Modern Fiction Studies,
24 (Winter 1978-79), 533-537.

   Although purportedly about The Grass is Sining,
   this essay in fact argues a more general case
   about Lessing's assimilation of Lawrentian
   description and character. Most striking are some
   specific passages which are compared for similar
   imagery. "if Doris Lessing has borrowed incident
   or description from Lawrence, it is because she was
   profoundly influenced by his philosophy." This
   essay may be usefully read along with the Magie
   essay (College English, 38, February 1977, 531-552)
   and the Spilka essay (Contemporary Literature, 16,
   Spring 1975, 218-240.)

355. Seligman, Dee. "Recent Lessing Seminar." Doris Lessing
Newsletter, 2 (Winter 1978), 12.

   A summary of Claire Sprague's "Dialectic and
   Counter-Dialectic in the Martha Quest Novels
   (later published in The Journal of Commonwealth
   Literature, 14, August 1979, 39-53) and of C. J.
   Bullock and Kay L. Steward's "Post-Party Politics:
   Doris Lessing's Novels of the Seventies." These
   papers were presented at the Berkshire Woman's
   Conference, August 1978, Mt. Holyoke College.

356. Lifson, Martha. "Structural Patterns in The Golden
Notebook." Michigan Papers in Women's Studies, 2, No. 4
(1978), 95-108.

   Claims that the basic structural unit in The
   Golden Notebook is 1) dream, 2) disillusionment
   and destruction of the dream, 3) chaos. "The
   pattern is a visible one and a source of excitement
   for the reader who perceives the tension between
   the expected pattern on the one hand and the
   seemingly free, chance, disparate, and multitudinous
   characters and events on the other; that is, between
   the structure of the novel and its obvious realism."
   Lifson describes accurately how Lessing "confuses the
   reader by presenting a shifting narrator, unstable
   or merging characters, and a non-chronological
   arrangement of events, all in order to undermine any

illusion of story and to bring structure, where her
meaning in fact resides, to the fore." Should be
read in conjunction with the following structural
essays on this novel: Carey (Contemporary Literature,
14, Autumn 1973, 437-457); Hynes (Iowa Review, 4,
Summer 1973, 100-113): Rubenstein (The Novelistic
Vision of Doris Lessing, Urbana: University of
Illinois Press, 1979), and Seligman ("The Autobiography of a New Consciousness," in 1975 dissertation, "The Autobiographical Fiction of Doris
Lessing.")

357. Millar, Helen J. "Doris Lessing's Short Stories: A
      Woman's Right to Choose?" Literature in North Queensland,
      6, No. 1 (1978), 24-38.

      Claims that "marriage, then, as Lessing writes
      about it, rarely lives up to its expectations in
      modern society." "Lessing's women, relying on
      marriage for happiness and fulfillment therefore
      remain victims of the institution." Lessing sees
      no middle path for the woman who gives up both her
      social and psychological freedom in marriage.
      Lessing is particularly adept at portraying the
      older woman who no longer finds sufficient outlet
      for her energy in the marital responsibilities.
      An interesting analysis of "Our Friend Judith" is
      offered which suggests she may be the only truly
      "free woman" in Lessing's work, although her
      freedom is dominated by her coldness and with-
      drawal from situations.

358. Millar, Helen J. "Doris Lessing's Short Stories: The
      Male's Point of View." Literature in North Queensland,
      6, No. 2 (1978), 42-53.

      Takes issue with Ellen Brooks' claim that in
      Lessing's stories men and women treat one another
      according to the sexist roles of oppressor and
      oppressed. Millar counters that Lessing's
      presentation is in fact "multi-faceted" and
      "stresses woman's vulnerability more than man's
      culpability." Millar shows that men are
      sympathetically portrayed as lonely and acting
      out of needs which are not inherently oppressive.
      Millar's remarks on "kindness" as a word of key
      import to Lessing are illuminating.

359. Stitzel, Judith. "Reading Doris Lessing." College
English, 40 (January 1979), 498-505.

This extremely important essay responds to
Magie's charge (College English, 38 February
1977) that Lessing is self-indulgent in her
mysticism. Stitzel contends that Lessing
urges us to think about thinking and that
her work encourages the reader to observe,
organize, and respond to all available input,
even that which is paradoxical. Reason need
not be simply a closed logical system based
upon non-contradiction, but should include
scrupulous attention to all types of experiences
which must be included in one's model of
knowing and being. Stitzel's reading of
"Report on the Threatened City" is most helpful.

360. Draine, Betsy. "Chaning Frames; Doris Lessing's
Memoirs of a Survivor." Studies in the Novel, 11
(Spring 1979), 51-63.

A useful article which deals directly with the
ending of the novel and its relation to the
two frames of reference, the realistic and the
mythic, of the narrative. Moreover, Draine
suggests that Lessing's failure at the ending
can best be judged by William James's three
criteria for "making the astounding believable."
Ultimately, the article discusses the
effectiveness of the form of Lessing's mystical
writing.

361. Seligman, Dee. "American Premiere of Each His Own
Wilderness." Doris Lessing Newsletter, 3 (Summer
1979), 13.

The first American performance of this play
was held in 1979, twenty-one years after its
original production.

362. Sprague, Claire. "Dialectic and Counter-Dialectic
in the Martha Quest Novels." The Journal of
Commonwealth Literature, 14 (August 1979), 39-53.

A sensitive account of the essential form of
the novel series. Claims that "two dialectics
are at work in sequence, one which we can
consider Marxist and the other in some part
Jungian and Eastern, but in more important part,
a creation of the author's and as such a liberation
from the parent structure." The Marxist
dialectic principle provides the essential rhythm
of repetition of the novel series: dying and
becoming, or the more organic methaphor of birth,
growth, death, and decay. The Marxist dialectic
also stresses the eternal conflict between dominant
forces and recessive forces, such as the inner-
outer city clash defined by Martha and by Mark
Coldridge. Lessing also creates a counter-dialectic
in her patterns of fours and fives which she super-
imposes on the patterns of twos and threes. Sprague
analyzes the structure of Children of Violence
in these terms and decides that five is used by
Lessing as the metaphoric opening out of the enclosed
space of four walls. The fifth volume is like the
golden notebook section and like the world behind
the wall in Memoirs. It is an opening out of
claustrophobia into a larger cosmic view.

363. Bourgeois, Susan. "Golden Notebooks: Patterns in
The Golden Notebook." Doris Lessing Newsletter, 3
(Winter 1979), 5, 12.

Anna Wulf listens to the music of Gerry Mulligan
in The Golden Notebook and in real life Mulligan
has composed a piece called "Golden Notebooks,"
in tribute to Lessing. Bourgeois analyzes the
stylistic similarities between the musical compo-
sition and its literary namesake.

364. Hoffeld, Laura and Natov, Roni. "The Summer Before the
Dark and The Memoirs of a Survivor: Lessing's New
Female Bondings." Doris Lessing Newsletter, 3 (Winter
1979), 11-12.

Examines the relationship between the older
female narrator and her adolescent counterpart.
The bond Kate forms with Maureen is a kind of
testing ground for her new way of seeing herself,"
while in Memoirs, the narrator's sense of self
is more fluid and her own growth, occurs by her
intense experience of Emily's past.

REFERENCES TO LESSING IN OTHER BOOKS

365. Wood, Neal. Communism and British Intellectuals. New York: Columbia University Press, 1959, p. 198, p. 202.

A reference to Lessing's contributing material to The Reasoner, an "unofficial communist journal."

366. Gindin, James. Postwar British Fiction: New Accents and Attitudes. Berkeley and Los Angeles: University of California Press, 1962, pp. 65-86.

A full survey of Lessing's work until 1962 organized around her sense of social responsibility. Gindin criticizes Lessing for lacking "a multiple awareness, a sense of comedy, a perception that parts of human experience cannot be categorized or precisely located, a human and intellectual depth. Intense commitment can cut off a whole dimension of human experience.

367. Taylor, John Russell. The Angry Theater: New British Drama. New York: Hill and Wang, 1962, p. 37, p. 145.

A bit of history of production on Lessing's dramatic work.

368. Karl, Frederick R. A Reader's Guide to the Contemporary English Novel. London: Thames and Hudson, 1963, pp. 281-283.

A summary of the major novels.

369. Allen, Walter. The Modern Novel in Britain and the United States. New York: E. P. Dutton and Co., 1964, pp. 176-177.

A summary of the major novels.

370. Schlueter, Paul. "The Free Woman's Commitment." In Contemporary British Novelists. Ed. Charles Shapiro. Carbondale and Edwardsville, Illinois: Southern Illinois University Press, 1965, pp. 48-62.

A brief survey of the themes of Lessing's fiction until 1965. The essay is useful only as an overview, and it is subsumed by Schlueter's later book on Lessing (#248).

371. Rabinovitz, Rubin. The Reaction Against Experiment in the English Novel 1950-1960. New York: Columbia University Press, 1967.

Lessing is mentioned in comparison with C.P. Snow, Kingsly Amis, and Angus Wilson.

372. Tucker, Martin. Africa in Modern Literature. New York: Frederick Ungar Co., 1967, pp. 175-183.

A brief comparison between Lessing and Olive Schreiner. An analysis of The Grass is Singing focuses on Lessing's particular use of the "servant problem" for this novel.

373. Wesker, Arnold. "Interview." In Theater at Work: Playwrights and Productions in the Modern British Theater. Ed. Charles Marowitz and Simon Trussler. New York: Hill and Wang, 1967, pp. 85-87.

A brief allusion to Lessing's, Wesker's, and other writers' development of Centre 42, a British home for the arts begun in the early 1960's.

374. Ellman, Mary. Thinking About Women. New York: Harcourt Brace Jovanovich, 1968, pp. 197-199.

375. Nicoll, Allardyce. "Somewhat in a New Dimension." In Contemporary Theater. Stratford-upon-Avon Studies. Ed. John Russell Brown and Bernard Harris. London: Edward Arnold Ltd., 1968, pp. 77-97.

A brief note about The Truth About Billy Newton suggests that Lessing's play is a "nostalgic groping back" to silent film.

376. Bergonzi, Bernard. The Situation of the Novel. Pittsburgh: University of Pittsburgh Press, 1970, pp. 200-204.

An interesting short piece on Lessing in which Bergonzi admits that The Golden Notebook is difficult to classify because "it dissolves the distinction between fact and direct autobiographical statement." Also suggests that The Golden Notebook reflects the idea that writing is primarily communication rather than making; hence, art is seen as distortion and evasion.

377. Robinson, Lillian S. "Who's Afraid of a Room of One's Own?" In The Politics of Literature. Ed. Louis Kampf and Paul Lauter. New York: Random House, 1970, pp. 354-407.

> A discussion of women writers and their work. Discussion of the weak cruel male as indigenous to Lessing's fiction, as well as to the fiction of many other women writers, provides useful insight, as does the repudiation of a "feminist" label by novelists such as Lessing.

378. Burgess, Anthony. The Novel Now: A Student's Guide to Contemporary Fiction. London: Faber and Faber, 1971, pp. 101-102, 107, 124, 160.

> Suggests that Lessing, being a crusader, should have written a manifesto rather than The Golden Notebook.

379. Lodge, David. The Novelist at the Crossroads. Ithaca, New York: Cornell University Press, 1971, p. 17, p. 24.

> A brief but useful reference to The Golden Notebook as a "problematic novel."

380. Thorpe, Michael. "Martha's Utopian Quest." In Commonwealth. Ed. Anna Rutherford. Aarhus, Denmark: Aarhus University, 1971, pp. 101-113.

> A description of The Four-Gated City which focuses on the Utopian quest of the novel. Thorpe believes that the Appendix offers "more than a vision to move, or pleasing fiction;...she is offering a vital but incommunicable experience."

381. Wellwarth, George. The Theater of Protest and Paradox. New York: New York University Press, 1971, pp. 289-291.

> Brief discussion of Each His Own Wilderness.

382. Morris, Robert K. "Children of Violence: Quest for Change. In Continuance and Change. Carbondale, Illinois: Southern Illinois Press, 1972, pp. 1-27.

An intelligent discussion of determinism in the
Children of Violence series. Morris concludes
that Lessing has "surrendered any pretense of
finding an answer" other than that the individual
and the collective will always be at odds. The
myth of the collective ideology failed after
World War II when ideological groups caused
separation from each other as human beings.
Morris provides interesting criticisms of the
series, including stereotyped female characters
and a failure on Lessing's part to maintain
ironic distance from Martha Quest.

383. Tindall, Gillian. "Doris Lessing:" In Contemporary
Novelists. Ed. James Vinton. New York: St. Martin's
Press, 1972.

A brief survey of all of Lessing's work until
1972.

384. Thompson, William Irwin. Passages About Earth. An
Exploration of the New Planetary Culture. New York:
Harper and Row, 1973, pp. 132-138; pp. 169-172.

A fascinating discussion of Briefing for a Descent
Into Hell from the perspective of "the etheric web"
of energy around the universe, from which "sensitive"
or "conscious" individuals intuit information,
including perhaps images of the collective unconscious.
Thompson has a fundamental affinity with Lessing's
work of the seventies and provides illumination
without literary history.

385. Christ, Carol. "Exploration with Doris Lessing in Quest of
The Four-Gated City. In Women and Religion. Ed. Judith
Plaskow and Joan Arnold. Missoula, Montana: Scholars
Press, 1974, pp. 31-61.

386. Miles, Rosalend. The Fiction of Sex: Themes and Functions
of Sex Difference in the Modern Novel. New York: Barnes
and Noble, 1974.

Intermittent references but without sustained
analysis to Lessing's novels. Good discussion of
Lessing's views of orgasm as depicted in The Golden
Notebook.

387. Kaplan, Sydney Janet. Feminine Consciousness in the Modern
      British Novel. Urbana: University of Illiois Press,
      1975, pp. 136-173.

          Discusses the feminine consciousness of Lessing
          as a visionary consciousness. Works discussed are
          The Golden Notebook, The Four-Gated City, Martha
          Quest, and Briefing. Argues that Lessing is
          marking the points of evolution away from the
          individual, egotistical, self-contained
          consciousness towards a communal consciousness
          in which individuals are merely receivers of
          universal energies of humanity and are part
          of Nature. Useful discussion of Anna Wulf's
          relation to Ella. Kaplan contends that only
          Lessing links the visionary process of her
          "feminine consciousness" to a real political
          context. This work is seminal and stands out
          as a coherent way of connecting Lessing's
          earlier work to her later work.

388. Spacks, Patricia Meyer. The Female Imagination. New
      York: Alfred A. Knopf, 1975.

          Discussion of Martha Quest, The Golden Notebook,
          The Four-Gated City, and The Summer Before the Dark
          which places these works in the context of work by
          other women writers. Spacks provides points of
          departure into controversial areas. Martha Quest
          is full of self-pity, and Spacks says that
          Lessing's anger with her heroine borders on "rage
          merging with despair." Spacks argues that the
          ending of Summer is not entirely satisfying
          for us or for Kate. The Golden Notebook is
          described as "narcissitic," because women's
          failure to achieve the masculine form of
          freedom is shown as their emblem of virtue.

389. Karl, Frederick. "The Four-Gaited Beast of the
      Apocalypse: Doris Lessing's The Four-Gated City."
      In Old Lines, New Forces. Ed. Robert K. Morris.
      Cranbury, New Jersey: Associated University Presses,
      1976, pp. 181-200.

One of the most illuminating articles on this novel.
Contends that the novel is Lessing's rewriting of
her feelings about the 1950's from the "vantage of
the late 1960's." Lynda and Mark Coldridge
represent two different directions for Martha--
the internal and the external worlds as focuses of
activity. Martha chooses Lynda's enclosed world,
which is not only a womb where self, will, and choice
are lost but also is a secular, non-sacred space in
which one may move on to a freer, more mysterious
space. Lessing's use of space is compared to
Harold Pinter's and her vision to that of Bosch.
Karl leaves open the question of whether Lessing's
apocalyptic focus is a capitulation to despair or
a fearless facing of the most terrible vision man
knows--the beast of the Apocalypse.

390. Watson, Barbara Bellow. "Leaving the Safety of Myth:
Doris Lessing's The Golden Notebook." In Old Lines,
New Forces. Ed. Robert K. Morris. Cranbury, New Jersey:
Associated University Presses, 1976, pp. 12-37.

A study of the causes of fragmentation expressed
in this novel. Among other things, fragmentation
is described as inherent in modern woman's position.
The puritan heritage of women and their dependence
on men for schedules, limitations, and shapes for
their lives is responsible for their fragmentation.

391. Cohen, Mary. "Out of the Chaos, a New Kind of Strength:
Doris Lessing's The Golden Notebook." In The Authority of
Experience. ed. Arlyn Diamond and Lee R. Edwards.
Amherst: University of Massachusetts Press, 1977,
pp. 160-178.

Asserts that Anna faces chaos and triumphs over
it in the "Golden Notebook" section of the novel;
however, the essay fails to explain how the
reintegration occurs. Anna represents our need
to reaffirm against despair.

392. Showalter, Elaine. A Literature of Their Own: British
Women Novelists from Bronte to Lessing. Princeton:
Princeton University Press, 1977, pp. 301-312.

Despite the book's subtitle, Showalter offers
only a brief discussion of Lessing. Showalter
analyzes Lessing's insistence that her work is
not feminist from the viewpoint of her class
consciousness, her aversion to the feminine
sensibility, and her alienation from her own
authentic female perspective. Concludes that
"either she will have to revise her apocalyptical
prophecies..., or confront, once again, the
struggling individual."

393. Gottlieb, Lois C. and Wendy Keitner. "Colonialism as Metaphor and Experience in The Grass is Singing, and Surfacing." In Awakened Conscience: Studies in Commonwealth Literature. Ed. C. D. Narasimhaiah. New Delhi: Sterling Press, 1978, pp. 307-314. Reprinted by Atlantic Highland, New Jersey: Humanities Press, 1978.

394. Morgan, Ellen. "Alienation of the Woman Writer in The Golden Notebook." in Feminist Criticism. Ed. Cheryl L. Brown and Karen Olson. Metuchen, New Jersey: Scarecrow Press, 1978, pp. 301-312.

    Reprint of essay found in Contemporary Literature, (#293).

395. Smith, David. Socialist Propaganda in the Twentieth-Century British Novel. London: MacMillan Press, 1978, pp. 148-151.

    One of the few pieces which deals with Lessing's work from the perspective of its socialist content. Retreat to Innocence comes "as close as any of her novels to delivering a direct, positive political message," even though the novel ends on a note of doubt concerning Jan Brod's efforts. A useful discussion for background to The Golden Notebook is Smith's analysis of the resignations of Communists from the Party after the Twentieth Congress and the invasion of Hungary. A description of the formation of the New Left Review, on whose editorial board Lessing once served, also is useful biographical background.

396. Rigney, Barbara Hill. Madness and Sexual Politics in the Feminist Novel. Madison: University of Wisconsin Press, 1978, pp. 65-91.

    Drawing heavily on R. D. Laing's psychoanalytic work, Rigney depicts the relationship between madness and the female condition as the oppressive society's sickness being played out in terms of restrictive sex roles. Good discussion of the doppelgänger as representative of the less sane half of the self. Asserts that the protagonist must find the mother within herself in order to achieve an integrated self. Comparisons between Lessing and Brontë, Woolf, and Margaret Atwood are useful.

397. Stewart, Grace. <u>A New Mythos: The Novels of the Artist as Heroine</u>. St. Albans, Vermont: Eden Press, 1978.

> Women writers operate within a group of patriarchal myths pertaining to their sex. The Faustian presentation of woman as Woman Eternal, forgiving, kind, and restorative is Goethe's contribution to the mythos. Anna Wulf in <u>The Golden Notebook</u> is caught between her "womanly" acceptance with all that the myth entails and her artistic nature which is inherently familiar with action, and creation through destruction. Anna rejects the old myths, but fails to construct new ones. She fears the formlessness of experience without the shaping power of the traditional myths. During her madness Anna experiences the anarchic quality of artistic creativity and the mythic quality of women as monsters of the deep. She rejects both myths as cages to her spirit. Stewart contends that Anna refuses artistic fulfillment which presupposes anarchy and destructiveness in favor of integration with the mainstream of British life. One might question whether Anna does "fear to act" and "decides not to write."

398. Swingewood, Alan. "Structure and Ideology in the Novels of Doris Lessing." In <u>The Sociology of Literature: Applied Studies</u>. Ed. Diana Laurenson. Keele, England: University of Keele, 1978. Sociological Review, Monograph 26.

> Lucien Goldmann's theory of the novel's form is used to analyze Lessing's career as a novelist. The move away from story telling to reportage is a function of the form of communication of the ruling class. The modernist movement from the traditional closed form of the novel to the open form, with its ambiguity of structure, value, and ending, occurs at moments of crisis within writers' social group. Swingewood breaks Lessing's career into three phases: a non-problematic realist phase; a problematic transitional phase characterized by a collective heroine and open form; and finally, "a return to realist narrative form but with a rejection of community and individual biography as basic constituent elements...." In any particular phase, one must refer to Lessing'g values, her view of the future, her ideological concept of selfhood, especially for women, at that particular historical time in order to grasp the meaning of a theme as it is handled in that particular text.

REVIEWS OF BOOKS ABOUT LESSING

399. Aycock, Linnea. "The Tree Outside the Window: A
Review." Doris Lessing Newsletter, 3 (Summer 1979),
14.

400. Bazin, Nancy T. "Review of Madness and Sexual
Politics in the Feminist Novel." Doris Lessing
Newsletter, 3 (Winter 1979), 6.

401. Burkom, Selma. "Michael Thorpe's Doris Lessing."
Research in African Lieteratures, 6 (Spring 1975),
128-133.

   Burkom is a critic long familiar with Lessing
   and hence, she provides more than a simple book
   review. This is really an essay on placing
   Lessing in the literary tradition. Burkom
   asserts she is a humanist and should be read
   in the context of Forster, George Eliot,
   Lawrence, and Coleridge.

402. Gage, Diane B. "The Relevance of History." Doris
Lessing Newsletter, 2 (Winter 1978), 4-5.

   A response rather than a review of M. C.
   Steele's monograph on Lessing as a historical
   observer (#252). Gage asserts that Lessing
   moves beyond historical observation to
   examining the act of observation itself, and
   should be criticized on these grounds alone.

403. Gindin, James. "Lessing Criticism." Contemporary
Literature, 14 (Autumn 1973), 586-589.

   A review of Paul Schlueter's The Novels of
   Doris Lessing.

404. Heinbockel, Madeline G. "Review of The City and the
Veld." Doris Lessing Newsletter, 2 (Summer 1978),
1, 10-11.

405. Krouse, Agate Nesaule. "Lessing in Feminist Literary
Criticism." Doris Lessing Newsletter, 2 (Summer
1978), 4, 8-9.

   A review of Sidney Janet Kaplan's Feminine
   Consciousness in the Modern British Novel,
   Ellen Moer's Literary Women, Patricia M.
   Spacks' The Female Imagination, Diamond and
   Edwards' The Authority of Experience, and
   Elaine Showalter's A Literature of Their Own.

406. Krouse, Agate Nesaule. "Review of The City and the
Veld." Criticism, 20 (Spring 1978), 216-218.

407. Rix, L. B. "Some Recent Criticism of Doris Lessing:
      Essay Review." Zambezia, 4 (December 1976), 103-106.

      A most interesting review of the Autumn 1973
      special issue on Lessing by Contemporary
      Literature and of Paul Schlueter's collection
      of her essays, A Small Personal Voice. This
      review is of particular interest because it
      presents a Rhodesian professor's perception
      of American criticism and its deficiencies.

408. Scholl, Diane G. "The Novels of Doris Lessing
      by Paul Schlueter." Christianity and Literature,
      23, No. 4, n.d., 39-45.

409. Schlueter, Paul. "Book Review of Rubenstein's
      The Novelistic Vision of Doris Lessing." Doris
      Lessing Newsletter, 3 (Winter 1979), 7-8.

410. Seligman, Dee. "A Critical Undertaking: Review
      of Latest Lessing Study." par rapport, 1 (Summer
      1978), 107-111.

      This essay reviews A City and the Veld and
      also surveys all of Lessing criticism
      during the seventies.

411. Seligman, Dee. "From an African Perspective."
      Doris Lessing Newsletter, 3 (Winter 1979), 3-4.

      A review of Michael Thorpe's book
      Doris Lessing's Africa.

412. Stitzel, Judith. "Book Review of Rubenstein's
      The Novelistic Vision of Doris Lessing." Doris
      Lessing Newsletter, 3 (Winter 1979), 7, 8-10.

      A long review which considers not only
      Rubenstein's book but also The Tree Outside
      the Window (Rose) and The City and the Veld
      (Singleton).

REVIEWS OF LESSING'S BOOKS

AFRICAN STORIES

413. Book List, 1 December 1965, p. 354.

414. Brophy, B. New Statesman, 67 (3 July 1964),
      p. 22.

415. Brown, E. H. Saturday Review, 23 October 1965,
      p. 67.

416. Casey, F. Christian Science Monitor, 6 January 1966, p. 11.

417. Cassity, T. Kenyon Review, 28 (March 1966), p. 279.

418. Choice, 2 (December 1965), p. 684.

419. Edelstein, J. M. Commonweal, 83 (28 January 1966), p. 514.

420. Ellman, Mary. Nation, 17 January 1966, p. 78.

421. Fleischer, L. Publishers Weekly, 189 (6 June 1966), p. 233.

422. Foster, P. Tablet (London), 218 (25 April 1964), p. 470.

423. Green, Martin. Book Week, 21 November 1965, p. 22.

424. The Guardian Weekly, 14 April 1973, p. 25.

425. Kirkus Review, 33 (1 September 1965), p. 939.

426. Kramer, Hilton. The New Leader, 25 October 1965, p. 21.

427. Levine, N. The Spectator, 17 April 1964, p. 522.

428. Moutafakis, G. J. Social Education, 30 (March 1966), p. 207.

429. Mudrick, Marvin. Hudson Review, 19 (Summer 1966), p. 307.

430. Newsweek, 18 October 1965, p. 128.

431. Peterson, V. Books Today, 3 (3 April 1966), p. 12.

432. Ready, W. Library Journal, 90 (15 December 1965), p. 5416.

433. Saturday Review, 24 September 1966, p. 40.

434. Scott, J. D. New York Times Book Review, 7 November 1965, p. 4.

435. Stille, E. Reporter, 34 (13 January 1966), p. 53.

436. Times Literary Supplement, 23 April 1964, p. 329.

BRIEFING FOR A DESCENT INTO HELL

437. America, 124 (22 May 1971), p. 548.

438. American Libraries, 2 (September 1971), p. 897.

439. Atlantic Monthly, 228 (August 1971), p. 89.

440. Best Sellers, 31 (1 May 1971), p. 72.

441. Books and Bookmen, 17 (November 1971), p. 44.

442. Books and Bookmen, 18 (September 1973), p. 138.

443. Book List, 67 (1 June 1971), p. 819.

444. Book World, 5 (28 February 1971), p. 1.

445. Book World, 5 (5 December 1971), p. 5.

446. Choice, 8 (June 1971), p. 551.

447. Christian Science Monitor, 18 March 1971, p. 11.

448. Commonweal, 97 (23 February 1973), p. 478.

449. De Mott, Benjamin. "Toward a More Human World."
     Saturday Review, 13 March 1971, pp. 25-27, 86-87.

450. Didion, Joan. New York Times Book Review, 14 March
     1971, p. 1, 39.

451. Economist, 241 (6 November 1971), p. viii.

452. Hudson Review, 24 (Summer 1971), p. 366.

453. Kirkus Review, 39 (1 January 1971), p. 21.

454. Library Journal, 96 (15 February 1971), p. 657.

455. Life, 70 (26 February 1971), p. 14.

456. Listener, 85 (22 April 1971), p. 524.

457. Maddocks, Melvin. "The White Bird of Truth."
     Time, 8 March 1971, p. 80.

458. McDowell, Frederick P. W. "Time of Plenty: Recent
     British Novels." Contemporary Literature, 13 (Summer
     1972), pp. 387-389.

459. Meyers, Jeffrey. Commonweal, 94 (7 May 1971), pp.
     220-221.

460. Nation, 213 (27 December 1971), p. 699.

461. National Observer, 10 (12 April 1971), p. 17.

462. New Leader, 54 (19 April 1971), p. 18.

463. New York Times, 10 March 1971, p. 41.

464. New York Times Book Review, 6 June 1971, p. 3.

465. New York Times Book Review, 5 December 1971, p. 82.

466. Observer, 18 April 1971, p. 32.

467. Observer, 5 August 1973, p. 25.

468. Pearson, Gabriel. The Guardian Weekly, 104
     (15 April 1971), p. 19.

469. Prescott, Peter. "Disk Jockey." Newsweek,
     12 April 1971, p. 118.

470. Publishers Weekly, 199 (18 January 1971), p. 46.

471. Sale, Roger. "Watchman, What of the Night?"
     New York Review of Books, 6 May 1971, pp. 13-17.

472. Thorpe, Michael. "Observation Ward." Encounter,
     37 (September 1971), p. 80.

473. Tindall, Gillian. "Charles the Mad." New Statesman,
     81 (16 April 1971), p. 535.

474. Times Literary Supplement, 16 April 1971, p. 437.

475. Waugh, Auberon. "On Female Novelists." Spectator,
     17 April 1971, p. 534.

CHILDREN OF VIOLENCE

(Martha Quest and A Proper Marriage)

476. Allen, Walter. "Martha the Rebel." New York Times
     Book Review, 15 November 1964. p. 5.

477. Allen, Walter. "Martha Quest and World War II."
     New York Times Book Review, 3 April 1966, p. 41.

478. Amis, Kingsley. Spectator, 8 October 1954, p. 450.

479. Bannon, B. A. Publishers Weekly, 189 (7 February
     1966), p. 91.

480. Bergonzi, Bernard. "In Pursuit of Doris Lessing."
     New York Review of Books, 11 February 1965, pp.
     12-14.

481. Best Sellers, 24 (15 December 1964), p. 377.

482. Book Week, 15 November 1964, p. 3.

483. Choice, 1 (February 1965), p. 555.

484. Corbett, E. P. J. America, 112 (2 January 1965),
     p. 21.

485. Dalton, Elizabeth. Kenyon Review, 27 (Summer 1965),
     pp. 572-573.

486. Davenport, G. National Review, 17 (23 February 1965),
     p. 155.

487. Davenport, John. Observer, 26 September 1954, p. 9.

488. Dienstag, Eleanor. "The Self-Analysis of Doris
     Lessing." New Republic, 152 (9 January 1965), pp.
     19-20.

489. Fremont-Smith, Eliot. "End Papers." New York Times
     Book Review, 17 December 1964, p. 39.

490. Graver, Lawrence. "The Commonplace Book of Doris
     Lessing." New Republic, 154 (2 April 1966), pp.
     27-29.

491. Hackett, A. Publishers Weekly, 190 (3 October 1966),
     p. 90.

492. Hicks, Granville. Saturday Review, 47 (14 November
     1964), p. 33.

493. Howe, Florence. "Doris Lessing's Free Women."
     Nation, 200 (11 January 1965), p. 34.

494. Kirkus Review, 33 (December 1965), p. 1205.

495. Marshall, Arthur Calder. British Broadcasting
     Corporation, 12 December 1954.

496. Mudrick, Marvin. Hudson Review, 18 (Spring 1965),
     p. 110.

497. Neiswender, R. Library Journal, 89 (15 December
     1964), p. 4932.

498. Newsweek, 7 December 1964, p. 106.

499. New Yorker, 40 (30 January 1965), p. 122.

500. Owen, Robert. "A Good Man is Hard to Find."
     Commentary, 39 (April 1965), pp. 79-82.

501. Peterson, V. Books Today, 3 January 1965, p. 5.

502. Peterson, V. Books Today, 3 April 1966, p. 12.

503. Time, 20 November 1964, p. 114.

504. Times Literary Supplement, 22 October 1954, p. 669.

505. Yanitelli, V. R. Best Sellers, 26 (15 April 1966), p. 33.

CHILDREN OF VIOLENCE

(A RIPPLE FROM THE STORM and LANDLOCKED)

506. Barker, Paul. "Doris Lessing: The Uses of Repetition." New Society, 24 June 1965, pp. 27-28.

507. Bradbury, M. Punch, 249 (14 July 1965), p. 66.

508. Byrom, B. Spectator, 25 June 1965, p. 826.

509. Carroll, J. M. Library Journal, 91 (15 January 1966), p. 278.

510. Choice, 3 (June 1966), p. 307.

511. Coleman, J. Observer, 20 June 1965, p. 27.

512. Corbett, E. P. American, 114 (2 April 1966), p. 450.

513. Graver, Lawrence. "The Commonplace Book of Doris Lessing. New Republic, 154 (2 April 1966), pp. 27-29.

514. Hicks, Granville. "All About a Modern Eve." Saturday Review, 49 (2 April 1966), pp. 31-32.

515. Howe, Florence. "Doris Lessing: The Child of Violence." Nation, 202 (13 June 1966), p. 716.

516. Schlueter, Paul. "Enduring Chronicle of Martha Quest." Panorama, Chicago Daily News, 2 April 1966, pp. 4-5.

517. Taubman, Robert. New Statesman, 70 (2 July 1965), p. 19.

518. Times Literary Supplement, 24 October 1958.

519. Times Literary Supplement, 24 June 1965, p. 533.

520. Tisdell, J. Books and Bookmen, 10 (July 1965), p. 26.

521. Walsh, J. National Observer, 25 April 1966, p. 20.

522. Yanitelli, V. R. Best Sellers, 26 (15 April 1966), p. 33.

523. Young, M. Book Week, 3 April 1966, p. 5.

EACH HIS OWN WILDERNESS

524. Alan Brian. Spectator, 200 (28 March 1958), p. 389.

525. Churchill, Caryl. "Not Ordinary, Not Safe." Twentieth Century, 148 (November 1960), pp. 443-451.

526. Seligman, Dee. "American Première of Each His Own Wilderness." Doris Lessing Newsletter, 3 (Summer 1979), p. 13.

527. The Times (London), 24 March 1958, p. 3.

528. Worsley, T. S. "The Do-Gooders." New Statesman, 55 (29 March 1958), p. 405.

FIVE

529. Books and Bookmen, 14 (August 1969), p. 41.

THE FOUR-GATED CITY

530. America, 121 (13 September 1969), p.171.

531. America, 121 (29 November 1969), p. 531.

532. American Libraries, 1 (January 1970), p. 91.

533. Atlantic Monthly, 224 (July 1969), p. 101.

534. Best Sellers, 29 (1 July 1969), p. 141.

535. Best Sellers, 30 (15 November 1970), p.360.

536. Books and Bookmen, 14 (August 1969), p. 8.

537. Booklist, 65 (15 July 1969), p. 1259.

538. Book World, 3 (25 May 1969), p. 8.

539. Book World, 3 (29 June 1969), p. 8.

540. Book World, 3 (7 December 1969), p. 16.

541. Burgess, Anthony. The Sunday Times (London),
     29 June 1969, p.55.

542. Choice, 6 (November 1969), p. 1222.

543. Christian Century, 87 (28 January 1970), p. 121.

544. Christian Science Monitor, 3 July 1969, p. 9, 11.

545. Commentary, 49 (January 1970), p. 85.

546. Commonweal, 90 (20 June 1969), p. 394.

547. Dalton, Elizabeth. "Quest's End." Commentary,
     49 (January 1970), pp. 85-87.

548. DeMott, Benjamin. "Toward a More Human World."
     Saturday Review, 13 March 1971, p. 86.

549. Ellman, Mary. "The Four-Gated City." New York Times
     Book Review, 18 May 1969, pp. 4-5.

550. Enright, D. J. "Shivery Games." New York Review of
     Books, 13 (31 July 1969), pp. 22-24.

551. Gordon, Jan B. "Prisons of Consciousness in
     Contemporary European Fiction." The Southern
     Review, 9 (Winter 1973), pp. 217-222.

552. The Manchester Guardian Weekly, 101 (20 December
     1969), p. 19.

553. Hardwick, Elizabeth. "Books." Vogue, 154 (July
     1969), p. 50.

554. Harper's, 239 (September 1969), p. 122.

555. Hudson Review, 22 (Fall 1969), p. 531.

556. Kirkus Review, 37 (15 March 1969), p. 332.

557. Library Journal, 94 (15 June 1969), p. 2486.

558. McDowell, Frederick P. W. "Recent British Fiction:
     Some Established Writers." Contemporary Literature,
     11 (Summer 1970), pp. 401-432.

559. Millar, Gavin. "End as a Seer." Listener, 82
     (3 July 1969), pp. 21-22.

560. Mortimer, Penelope. The Manchester Guardian Weekly,
     101 (3 July 1969), p. 15.

561. Nation, 209 (11 August 1969), p. 116.

562. National Observer, 8 (9 June 1969), p. 23.

563. New Leader, 52 (7 July 1969), p. 13.

564. New Statesman, 78 (4 July 1969), p. 19.

565. Newsweek, 73 (26 May 1969), p. 117.

566. New Yorker, 45 (14 June 1969), p. 114.

567. New York Times, 118 (15 May 1969), p. 45.

568. New York Times Book Review, 18 May 1969, p. 4.

569. New York Times Book Review, 8 June 1969, p. 56.

570. Oates, Joyce Carol. "Last Children of Violence."
     Saturday Review, 52 (17 May 1969), p. 48.

571. Observer, 29 June 1969, p. 24.

572. Publishers Weekly, 52 (17 May 1969), p. 48.

573. Rabin, Jonathan. "Mrs. Lessing's Diary." London
     Magazine, 9 (September 1969), pp. 111-115.

574. Spectator, 223 (5 July 1969), p. 118.

575. Thorpe, Michael. "Real and Ideal Cities." Journal
     of Commonwealth Literature, July 1970, pp. 119-122.

576. Time, 94 (25 July 1969), p. 75.

577. Times Literary Supplement, 514 (3 July 1969), p. 720.

THE GOLDEN NOTEBOOK

578. Bliven, Naomi. "It's Not a Woman's World." New
     Yorker, 1 June 1963, pp. 114-119.

579. Books and Bookmen, 18 (September 1973), p. 138.

580. Booklist, 59 (1 September 1962), p. 31.

581. Bowen, John. Punch, 9 May 1962, p. 733.

582. Britten, Anne. "Doris Lessing's Whirlwind." Books
     and Bookmen, May 1962.

583. Brooks, Jeremy. "Doris Lessing's Chinese Box."
     The Sunday Times (London), 15 April 1962, p. 32.

584. Buckler, Ernest. New York Times, 1 July 1962,
     pp. 1-4.

585. Cowley, Malcolm. "Future Notebook." Saturday Review, 28 June 1975, pp. 23-24.

586. Crutwell, Patrick. Hudson Review, 15 (Winter 1962-63), p. 591.

587. Didion, Joan. New York Times Book Review, 14 March 1971, p. 1, pp. 38-39.

588. Dolbier, Maurice. New York Herald Tribune, 29 June 1962, p. 17.

589. Emerson, Joyce. Bookman, May 1962.

590. Fruchter, Norman. Studies on the Left, Spring 1964.

591. The Guardian, 8 June 1962, p. 7.

592. Hicks, Granville. "Complexities of a Free Woman." Saturday Review, 45 (30 June 1962), p. 16.

593. Hope, Francis. "Heroine of Our Time." Observer, 15 April 1962.

594. Howe, Florence. "Doris Lessing's Free Women." Nation, 200 (11 January 1965), pp. 34-37.

595. Howe, Irving. "Neither Compromise Nor Happiness." New Republic, 147 (15 December 1962), pp. 17-20.

596. Jameson, Storm. "Love's Labours Exposed." Spectator, 7180 (4 February 1966), p. 134.

597. Kirkus Review, 30 (1 May 1962), p. 432.

598. Kramer, H. New Leader, 48 (25 October 1965), p. 21.

599. Library Journal, 96 (1 September 1971), p. 2591.

600. Magrid, Nora. Commonweal, 77 (5 October 1962), p. 53.

601. McDowell, Frederick P. W. "The Devious Involutions of Human Character and Emotions: Reflections on Some Recent British Novels." Wisconsin Studies in Contemporary Literature, 4 (Autumn 1963), pp. 346-350.

602. Mathew, Ray. London Magazine, June 1962, p. 95.

603. Mitchell, Julian. Spectator, 20 April 1962, p. 518.

604. Neiswender, Rosemary. Library Journal, 87 (15 June 1962), p. 2399.

605. Newsweek, 2 July 1962, p. 82.

606. New York Times Book Review, 1 July 1962, p. 4.

607. Nordell, Roderick. "Theme and Technique." Christian Science Monitor, 5 July 1962, p. 11.

608. Nott, Kathleen. "Counterpoint to Lawrence." Time and Tide, 43 (26 April 1962), p. 33.

609. Observer, 20 May 1973, p. 33.

610. Prescott, Orville. New York Times, 29 June 1962, p. 25.

611. Publishers Weekly, 193 (29 January 1968), p. 100.

612. Saturday Night, 84 (August 1969), p. 33.

613. Scannell, Vernon. The Listener, 3 May 1962, p. 785.

614. Spectator, 20 April 1962, p. 518.

615. Taubman, Robert. "Free Women." New Statesman, 63 (20 April 1962), p. 569.

616. Taubman, Robert. "Near Zero." New Statesman, (8 November 1963), pp. 653-654.

617. Taubman, Robert. "Free Women." In On Contemporary Literature. Ed. Richard Kostelanetz. New York: Avon Books, 1964, pp. 402-403.

618. Time, 80 (13 July 1962), p. 86.

619. Times Literary Supplement, 3139 (27 April 1962), p. 280.

620. de Toledano, Ralph. National Review, 25 September 1962, p. 235.

621. White, Ellington. Kenyon Review, 24 (Autumn 1962), p. 750.

GOING HOME

622. Bacon, M. H. Antioch Review, 25 (Fall 1965), p. 447.

623. Miller, C. Saturday Review, 51 (23 March 1968), p. 45.

624. Observer, 25 November 1973, p. 35.

625. Publishers Weekly, 193 (29 January 1968), p. 98.

THE GRASS IS SINGING

626. Allen, Walter. "Her Early Novels." In On
Contemporary Literature. Ed. Richard Kostelanetz.
New York: Avon Books, 1964, pp. 400-401.

627. Antioch Review, 34 (Spring 1976), p. 377.

628. Church, Richard. John O'London's, 17 March 1950.

629. Goven, Christine N. "Stumbling, Groping, Pitiable
People." Saturday Review, 33 (21 October 1950), p.
44.

630. Johnson, Pamela Hansford. Daily Telegraph (London),
14 March 1950.

631. Jones, Ernest. "Some Recent Fiction." Nation, 171
(23 September 1950), p. 273.

632. Kirkus Review, 18 (1 July 1950), p. 366.

633. Laski, Marghanita. "Fiction." Spectator, 184 (31
March 1950), p. 442, 444.

634. The Manchester Guardian, 17 March 1950, p. 4.

635. New Republic, 172 (21 June 1975), p. 21.

636. New York Times, 10 September 1950, p. 4.

637. New York Review of Books, 22 (17 July 1975), p. 38.

638. New York Herald Tribune Book Review, 10 September
1950, p. 8.

639. New Yorker, 26 (16 September 1950), p. 119.

640. Sewanee Review, 84 (April 1976), p. R 36.

641. Thorpe, Michael. "The Grass is Singing." Literary
Half-Yearly, 19 (1978), pp. 17-26.

642. Time, 56 (18 September 1950), p. 122.

643. Times Literary Supplement, 2115 (14 April 1950), p.
225.

644. Walbridge, Earle. "The Grass is Singing." Library
Journal, 75 (1 September 1950), p. 1408.

645. White, Antonia. "New Novels." New Statesman, 39 (1
April 1950), pp. 378-379.

646. Wyndham, Francis. Observer, 19 March 1950.

THE HABIT OF LOVING

647. Booklist, 55 (1 September 1958), p. 22.

648. Book World (Washington Post), 19 September 1976, p. H3.

649. Chicago Sunday Tribune, 13 July 1958, p. 3.

650. Fuller, Roy. London Magazine, 5(March 1958), P. 69.

651. Gordimer, Nadine. Africa South, 2 (July–September 1958), pp. 124-126.

652. Heinemann, Margot. Daily Worker (London), 2 January 1958.

653. Johnson, Pamela Hansford. New Statesman, 54 (23 November 1957), p. 500.

654. Kirkus Review, 26 (15 May 1958), p. 364.

655. Library Journal, 83 (July 1958), p. 2052.

656. Maddocks, Melvin. "Amor Vincent Omnia?" Time, 103 (20 May 1974), p. K11, 90.

657. The Manchester Guardian, 26 November 1957, p. 4.

658. Michaelis–Jena, Ruth. Weekly Scotsman, 11 January 1958.

659. New York Herald Tribune Book Review, 13 July 1958, p. 4.

660. New York Times, 20 July 1958, p. 4.

661. Observer, 24 April 1966, p. 22.

662. Sachs, Joseph. "The Short Stories of Gordimer, Lessing and Bosman." Trek, 15 (November 1951), pp. 15-16.

663. Spectator, 22 November 1957, p. 706.

664. Symons, Julian. Evening Standard (London), 19 November 1957.

665. Time, 72 (14 July 1958), p. 88.

666. Times Literary Supplement, 29 November 1957, p. 717.

IN PURSUIT OF THE ENGLISH

667. Baro, Gene. New York Herald Tribune Lively Arts, 19 March 1961, p. 31.

668. Booklist, 57 (15 March 1961), p. 447.

669. Bowers, Faubion. Saturday Review, 44 (25 March 1961), p. 25.

670. Bradbury, Malcolm. New York Times Book Review, 5 March 1961, p. 4.

671. Corbett, Hugh. Books Abroad, Spring 1962, p. 206.

672. Cosman, Max. Commonweal, 74 (14 April 1961), p. 86.

673. Dangerfield, George. Nation, 192 (15 April 1961), p. 324.

674. Findlater, Richard. Evening Standard (London), 14 June 1960.

675. Fraser, R. A. San Francisco Chronicle, 5 March 1961, p. 26.

676. Gilliat, Penelope. Spectator, 20 May 1960, p. 740.

677. Glick, Nathan. New Leader, 27 November 1961, p. 29.

678. Goldsborough, Diane. Tamarack Review, Spring 1961, p. 101.

679. Gravel, George E. America, 18 March 1961, p. 796.

680. Jones, Mervyn. Observer, 8 May 1960, P. 23.

681. Lambert, G. W. The Sunday Times (London), 5 June 1960, p. 16 Magazine Section.

682. Laski, Marghanita. News Chronicle (London), 11 May 1960.

683. Mair, L. P. The Listener, 26 May 1960, p. 945.

684. Mudrick, Marvin. Hudson Review, 14 (Summer 1961), p. 289.

685. New Yorker, 37 (2 December 1961), p. 234.

686. Potts, Paul. London Magazine, September 1960, p. 82.

687. Price, R. G. G. Punch, 7 September 1970, p. 357.

688. Rosselli, John. The Guardian, 12 May 1960, p. 6.

689. Springfield Republican, 12 March 1961, p. 4D.

690. Time, 77 (3 March 1961), p. 96.

691. Times Literary Supplement, 26 May 1960, p. 12.

692. Times Literary Supplement, 1 July 1960, p. 416.

693. Ware, Jean. Liverpool Daily Post, 1 June 1960.

694. Waterhouse, Keith. New Statesman, 59 (4 June 1960), p. 832.

A MAN AND TWO WOMEN

695. Auchincloss, Eve. New York Review of Books, 1 (17 October 1963), p. 5.

696. Book Week, 13 October 1963, p. 16.

697. Deane, Peter. New York Herald Tribune, 14 October 1963, p. 16.

698. Dolbier, Maurice. New York Herald Tribune, 14 October 1963, p. 14.

699. Gindin, James. Saturday Review, 46 (23 November 1963), p. 42.

700. Hamilton, A. Books and Bookmen, 10 (April 1965), p. 55.

701. Howard, R. Partisan Review, 32 (Winter 1969), p. 117.

702. Howes, B. The Massachusetts Review, 5 (Spring 1964), p. 583.

703. Kauffman, Stanley. "The World is Much with Her." New York Times Book Review, 13 October 1963, p. 4.

704. Kauffman, Stanley. "Literature of the Sixties." Wilson Library Bulletin, 39 (May 1965), pp. 751-752.

705. London Times Weekly Review, 24 October 1963, p. 13.

706. Mudrick, Marvin. Hudson Review, 17 (Spring 1974), p. 110.

707. Newsweek, 62 (14 October 1963), p. 118.

708. Pickrel, Paul. Harper's, 227 (November 1963), p. 130.

709. Pollock, Venetia. Punch, 245 (13 November 1963), p. 722.

710. Saturday Review, 48 (20 November 1965), p. 40.

711. Schott, Webster. "The Purpose of Life." Nation,
     197 (14 December 1963), p. 419.

712. Stiles, Patricia. Library Journal, 88 (15 November
     1963), p. 4396.

713. Sullivan, Richard. Chicago Sun Tribune Magazine of
     Books, 3 November 1963, p. 3.

714. Taubman, Robert. "Near Zero." New Statesman,
     66 (8 November 1963), p. 653.

715. Time, 82 (18 October 1963), p. 123.

716. Times Literary Supplement, 18 October 1963, p. 821.

717. Wardle, Irving. "Happiness Isn't Allowed."
     Observer, 6 October 1963.

THE MEMOIRS OF A SURVIVOR

718. Ackroyd, Peter. The Spectator, 233 (21 December
     1974), p. 792.

719. America, 133 (15 November 1975), p. 332.

720. Best Sellers, 35 (July 1975), p. 82.

721. Booklist, 72 (1 September 1975), p. 25.

722. Book World, 15 June 1975, p. 3.

723. Bryden, Ronald. "On the Move." New Statesman,
     88 (6 December 1974), pp. 826-827.

724. Canadian Forum, 55 (December 1975), p. 56.

725. Choice, 12 (September 1975), p. 843.

726. Christian Science Monitor, 67 (12 June 1975), p. 22.

727. Clemons, Walter. "Things to Come." Newsweek, 16 June
     1975, pp. 75-76.

728. Commonweal, 102 (1 August 1975), p. 315.

729. Contemporary Review, 226 (April 1975), p. 213.

730. Critic, 38 (August 1979), p. 6.

731. Dinage, Rosemary. "In the Disintegrating City."
     New York Review of Books, 22 (17 July 1975), pp.
     38-39.

732. English Journal, 67 (December 1978), p. 83.

733. Garis, Leslie. "Through a Wall Darkly." Book World-
     Washington Post, 15 June 1975, p. 3.

734. Howard, Maureen. New York Times Book Review, 8 June
     1975, p. 1.

735. Kirkus Review, 43 (1 April 1975), p. 399.

736. Kliatt Paperback Book Guide, 11 (Winter 1977), p. 5.

737. Levy, Paul. Books and Bookmen, 20 (April 1975), p.
     58.

738. Library Journal, 100 (July 1975), p. 1346.

739. Listener, 93 (23 January 1975), p. 126.

740. Ludwig, Linda. "More Lessing." Literary Quarterly,
     15 May 1975, p. 13.

741. Maddocks, Melvin. "Ghosts and Portents." Time,
     105 (16 June 1975), p. 79.

742. McDowell, Judith H. "Doris Lessing: The Memoirs of
     a Survivor." World Literature Written in English,
     15 (November 1976), pp. 323-326.

743. Nation, 221 (6 September 1975), p. 184.

744. National Observer, 14 (19 July 1975), p. 21.

745. National Review, 18 (30 April 1976), p. 462.

746. New York Times, 124 (2 June 1975), p. 23.

747. New York Times Book Review, 7 December 1975, p. 62.

748. Newsweek, 85 (16 June 1975), p. 21.

749. New Yorker, 51 (2 June 1975), p. 109.

750. Observer, 15 December 1974, p. 26.

751. Observer, 11 July 1976, p. 21.

752. Progressive, 39 (August 1975), p. 45.

753. Psychology Today, 9 (June 1975), p. 12.

754. Publishers Weekly, 207 (28 April 1975), p. 39.

755. Publishers Weekly, 210 (23 August 1976), p. 74.

756. Rubenstein, Roberta. The New Republic, 172 (21 June 1975), p. 21.

757. Sale, Roger. Hudson Review, 28 (Winter 1975-1976), p. 616.

758. Saturday Review, 2 (28 June 1975), p. 23.

759. Sewanee Review, 84 (April 1976), p. R36.

760. The Sunday Times (London), 8 December 1974, p. 38.

761. The Sunday Times (London), 13 June 1976, p. 39.

762. Times Literary Supplement, 13 December 1974, p. 1405.

763. West Coast Review of Books, 3 (March 1977), p. 55.

MR. DOLINGER

764. Observer, 13 July 1958, p. 15.

765. Tynan, Kenneth. The Times (London), 8 July 1958, p. 5.

PARTICULARLY CATS

766. Booklist, 64 (1 September 1967), p. 29.

767. Books and Bookmen, 13 (December 1967), p. 50.

768. Changing Times, 33 (April 1979), p. 37.

769. Cook, R. Harper's Monthly, 235 (July 1967), p. 95.

770. Jacobson, E. Books Today, 4 (30 April 1967), p. 5.

771. Kirkus Review, 35 (15 March 1967), p. 389.

772. Kliatt's Paperback Book Guide, 13 (Spring 1979), p. 56.

773. New York Times Book Review, 21 January 1979, p. 37.

774. Observer, 20 May 1979, p. 37.

775. Publishers Weekly, 191 (13 March 1967), p. 57.

776. Radosta, J. S. New York Times, 116 (6 May 1967),
     p. 29.

777. Willis, K. T. Library Journal, 92 (15 April 1967),
     p. 1635.

PLAY WITH A TIGER

778. Illustrated London News, 240 (7 April 1962), p. 554.

779. New Statesman, 63 (30 March 1962), p. 462.

780. New Yorker, 40 (9 January 1965), p. 86.

781. Spectator, 208 (30 March 1962), p. 398.

TO ROOM NINETEEN

782. Books and Bookmen, 23 (September 1978), p. 55.

783. Contemporary Review, 233 (October 1978), p. 213.

784. Encounter, 51 (September 1978), p. 73.

785. Ferguson, Mary Anne. "Sexist Images of Women in
     Literature." In Female Studies V. Ed. Rae Lee
     Siporin. Pittsburgh: KNOW, 1972, pp. 77-83.

786. New Statesman, 95 (30 June 1978), p. 888.

787. Observer, 9 July 1978, p. 25.

788. Spectator, 240 (1 July 1978), p. 28.

789. Times Literary Supplement, 23 June 1978, p. 695.

A SMALL PERSONAL VOICE

790. Booklist, 71 (15 November 1974), p. 315.

791. Carnes, Valerie. Doris Lessing Newsletter, 1 (Winter
     1976), p. 2, p. 11.

792. Christian Science Monitor, 66 (23 October 1974), p.
     13.

793. Crain, Jane Larkin. Saturday Review, 2 (21 September
     1974), p. 27.

794. Critic, 33 (January 1975), p. 58.

795. Kirkus Review, 42 (15 July 1974), p. 783.

796. Library Journal, 99 (15 October 1974), p. 2605.

797. Lindborg, Henry J. "Search for Unity." New Republic,
    171 (5 October 1974), p. 22.

798. Nation, 220 (18 January 1975), p. 56.

799. Publishers Weekly, 206 (26 August 1974), p. 301.

800. Publishers Weekly, 208 (14 July 1975), p. 62.

801. Sale, Roger. New York Times Book Review, 22 September
    1974, p. 4.

802. Sewanee Review, 84 (April 1976), p. R36.

803. Village Voice, 19 (17 October 1974), p. 31.

THE STORY OF A NON-MARRYING MAN

804. Books and Bookmen, 18 (December 1972), p. 98.

805. Books and Bookmen, 18 (January 1973), p. 28.

806. Contemporary Review, 222 (January 1973), p. 46.

807. Hope, Francis. Observer, 24 September 1972, p. 37.

808. Listener, 88 (24 September 1972), p. 376.

809. New Statesman, 84 (22 September 1972), p. 402.

810. Observer, 31 August 1975, p. 18.

811. Spectator, 229 (23 December 1972), p. 1010.

812. Times Literary Supplement, 22 September 1972,
    p. 1087.

813. The Times (London), 28 September 1972, p. 13.

814. The Times Educational Supplement, 17 October
    1975, p. 26.

STORIES

815. Best Sellers, 38 (October 1978), p. 205.

816. Booklist, 74 (1 May 1978), p. 1412.

817. Book World–Washington Post, 10 December 1978, p. E1.

818. Book World–Washington Post, 14 May 1978, p. G5.

819. Choice, 15 (September 1978), p. 870.

820. Christian Science Monitor, 70 (5 June 1978), p. 30.

821. Dinnage, Rosemary. "Before Her Time." New York Review of Books, 28 September 1977, pp. 12–14.

822. Kirkus Review, 46 (1 April 1978), p. 397.

823. Library Journal, 103 (15 May 1978), p. 1082.

824. Ms., 7 (July 1978), p. 32.

825. Natonal Review, 30 (15 September 1978), p. 1155.

826. New Boston Review, 4 (December 1978), p. 21.

827. Newsweek, 91 (22 May 1978), p. 75.

828. Observer, 17 December 1978, p. 33.

829. Publishers Weekly, 213 (3 April 1978), p. 69.

830. Saturday Review, 5 (27 May 1978), p. 54.

831. Tiger, Virginia. "Lessing's Stories." Doris Lessing Newsletter, 3 (Winter 1979), pp. 13–14.

832. The Sunday Times (London), 16 July 1978, p. 41.

833. The Sunday Times (London), 26 November 1978, p. 39.

834. Time, 111 (19 June 1978), p. 85.

835. Virginia Quarterly Review, 54 (Autumn 1978), p. 136.

836. Village Voice, 23 (2 October 1978), p. 127.

THE SUMMER BEFORE THE DARK

837. America, 129 (1 September 1973), p. 126.

838. America, 129 (17 November 1973), p. 381.

839. Atlantic Monthly, 231 (June 1973), p. 116.

840. Best Sellers, 33 (1 July 1973), p. 154.

841. Best Sellers, 34 (15 December 1974), p. 428.

842. Books and Bookmen, 18 (July 1973), p. 113.

843. Book World–Washington Post, 7 (20 May 1973), p. 3.

844. Book World–Washington Post, 7 (3 June 1973), p. 14.

845. Book World–Washington Post, 7 (9 December 1973), p. 2.

846. Book World–Washington Post, 22 December 1974, p. 3.

847. Book World–Washington Post, 3 November 1974, p. 4.

848. Broyard, Anatole. New York Times, 7 May 1973, p. 37.

849. Choice, 10 (October 1973), p. 1195.

850. Christian Science Monitor, 23 May 1973, p. 11.

851. Commentary, 56 (September 1973), p. 85.

852. Economist Survey, 247 (5 May 1973), p. 6.

853. The Guardian Weekly, 108 (14 April 1973), p. 25.

854. The Guradian Weekly, 108 (12 May 1973), p. 26.

855. Hardwick, Elizabeth. New York Times Book Review,
13 May 1973, pp. 1–2.

856. Hendin, Josephine. "Doris Lessing: The Phoenix
Midst Her Fires." Harper's, 246 (June 1973),
pp. 83–86.

857. Hudson Review, 26 (Fall 1973), p. 545.

858. Jong, Erica. "Everwoman Out of Love?" Partisan
Review, 40, No. 3 (1973), pp. 500–503.

859. Kirkus Review, 41 (1 March 1973), p. 268.

860. Library Journal, 98 (15 March 1973), p. 886.

861. Listener, 89 (10 May 1973), p. 623.

862. Lurie, Alsion. "Wise Women." New York Review of
Books, 20 (14 June 1973), p. 18.

863. Manning, Margaret. "Doris Lessing's Belief in
Survival." Atlantic Monthly, 231 (June 1973),
pp. 116–118.

864. Nation, 217 (27 August 1973), p. 151.

865. National Observer, 12 (9 June 1973), p. 23.

866. New Leader, 56 (11 June 1973), p. 16.

867. New Republic, 168 (12 May 1973), p. 28.

868. New Statesman, 85 (4 May 1973), p. 665.

869. Newsweek, 81 (14 May 1973), p. 118.

870. New York Review of Books, 20 (14 June 1973), p. 18.

871. New York Times, 7 May 1973, p. 37.

872. New York Times Book Review, 13 May 1973, p. 1.

873. New York Times Book Review, 10 June 1973, p. 40.

874. New York Times Book Review, 2 December 1973, p. 1.

875. New York Times Book Review, 13 October 1974, p. 44.

876. New York Times Book Review, 10 November 1974, p. 39.

877. New York Times Book Review, 15 January 1978, p. 3.

878. Observer, 6 May 1973, p. 37.

879. Observer, 31 August 1975, p. 18.

880. Progressive, 37 (August 1973), p. 47.

881. Psychology Today, 8 (February 1975), p. 114.

882. Publishers Weekly, 203 (26 March 1973), p. 67.

883. Publishers Weekly, 205 (13 May 1974), p. 60.

884. Shapiro, Susan. "The Summer Before the Dark." Crawdaddy, November 1973, pp. 89-90.

885. Sissman, L. E. New Yorker, 49 (9 June 1973), p. 113.

886. The Times (London), 3 May 1973, p. 10.

887. The Sunday Times (London), 6 July 1975.

888. Time, 101 (21 May 1973), p. 99.

889. Time, 102 (31 December 1973), p. 56.

890. Times Literary Supplement, 4 May 1973, p. 489.

891. Widmann, R. L. "Lessing's The Summer Before the Dark." Contemporary Literature, 14 (Autumn 1973), pp. 582-585.

892. World, 2 (31 July 1973), p. 33.

THE SUN BETWEEN THEIR FEET

893. The Guardian Weekly, 108 (14 April 1973), p. 25.

894. New Statesman, 85 (4 May 1973), p. 665.

THE TEMPTATION OF JACK ORKNEY

895. America, 127 (7 October 1972), p. 265.

896. Atlantic Monthly, 230 (December 1972), p. 144.

897. Best Sellers, 32 (1 February 1973), p. 488.

898. Best Sellers, 34 (15 December 1974), p. 428.

899. Books and Bookmen, 23 (September 1978), p. 55.

900. Booklist, 69 (1 January 1973), p. 428.

901. Book World—Washington Post, 3 November 1974, p. 4.

902. Book World—Washington Post, 3 December 1972, p. 5.

903. Choice, 10 (March 1973), p. 94.

904. Christian Science Monitor, 65 (10 January 1973), p. 10.

905. Duchene, Anne. "The Steps to the Pulpit." Times Literary Supplement, 23 June 1978, p. 695.

906. Encounter, 51 (September 1978), p. 73.

907. Graver, Lawrence. New York Times Book Review, 29 October 1972, p. 4, 12.

908. Hudson Review, 26 (Spring 1973), p. 234.

909. Kirkus Review, 40 (15 August 1972), p. 970.

910. Library Journal, 97 (15 September 1972), p. 2861.

911. Life, 73 (17 November 1972), p. 26.

912. National Observer, 11 (14 October 1972), p. 21.

913. National Review, 24 (22 December 1972), p. 4413.

914. New Statesman, 95 (30 June 1978), p. 888.

915. New Republic, 167 (2 December 1972), p. 24.

916. New York Times, 122 (21 October 1972), p. 31.

917. New York Times Book Review, 10 November 1974, p. 39.

918. New York Times Book Review, 3 December 1972, p. 80.

919. Oates, Joyce Carol. "So Much for the Search for Truth." Book World-Washington Post, 22 October 1972, p. 4, p. 13.

920. Observer, 9 July 1978, p. 25.

921. Psychology, Today, 5 (February 1973), p. 91.

922. Psychology Today, 8 (February 1975), p. 114.

923. Publishers Weekly, 202 (18 September 1972), p. 71.

924. Publishers Weekly, 205 (13 May 1974), p. 60.

925. Rabinowitz, Dorothy. World, 24 October 1972, p. 53.

926. Rose, Ellen Cronan. "Don't Review, Don't Go On TV." Nation, 18 January 1975, pp. 56-57.

927. Sale, Roger. New York Review of Books, 19 (25 January 1973), p. 43.

928. Saturday Review, 55 (2 December 1972), p. 80.

929. Spectator, 240 (1 July 1978), p. 28

930. The Times (London), 13 July 1978, p. 11.

931. Time, 100 (23 October 1972), p. 106.

932. Time, 101 (1 January 1973), p. 61.

933. Times Literary Supplement, 23 June 1978, p. 695.

THIS WAS THE OLD CHIEF'S COUNTRY

934. Booklist, 49 (1 September 1952), p. 13.

935. The Guardian Weekly, 108 (14 April 1973), p. 25.

936. Laski, Marghanita. Observer, 22 April 1951. p, 7.

937. Laski, Marghanita. Observer, 30 December 1951. p. 7.

938. New Statesman, 85 (4 May 1973), p. 665.

939. New York Herald Tribune Book Review, 22 June 1952, p. 4.

940. New York Times, 13 July 1952, p. 16.

941. Publishers Weekly, 161 (2 February 1952), p. 706.

942. Saturday Review, 35 (2 August 1952), p. 19.

943. Snow, C. P. The Sunday Times (London), 8 April 1951, p. 3.

944. Spring, Howard. Country Life (London), 20 April 1951, p. 1225.

945. Street, Allen. Current Literature (London), April 1951.

946. Strong, L. A. G. Spectator, 185 (4 May 1951), p. 598.

947. Symons, Julian. Manchester Evening News, 12 April 1951.

948. Times Literary Supplement, 11 May 1951, p. 289.

949. Wintringham, Margaret. Time and Tide, 28 July 1951, p. 730.

THE TRUTH ABOUT BILLY NEWTON

950. New Statesman, 59 (23 January 1960), p. 102.

951. Page, Malcolm. "Lessing's Unpublished Plays." Doris Lessing Newsletter, 1 (Fall 1977), p. 3, p. 6.

952. Pryce-Jones. Observer, 24 January 1960, p. 21.

953. The Tribune (London), 22 January 1960, p. 11.

WINTER IN JULY

954. Observer, 21 August 1966, p. 14.

MODERN LANGUAGE ASSOCIATION PAPERS ON LESSING

These papers are generally available from the person who chaired the session; their current address is best checked in the September issue of PMLA.

1971--Chair: Paul Schlueter. Title: "The Fiction of Doris Lessing."

955. Ashley, Leonard R. N.: "Children of Violence as a 'Golden Notebook': The Writing of Doris Lessing."

956. Burkom, Selma R. "Wholeness as Hieroglyph: Lessing's Typical Mode and Meaning."

957. Marchino, Lois. "The Search for Self in the Novels of Doris Lessing."

958. Smith, Diane S. "Ant Imagery as Thematic Device in the Children of Violence Series."

1972--Chair: Lois Marchino. Title: "The Fiction of Doris Lessing."

959. Pratt, Annis. "The Contrary Structure of Doris Lessing's The Golden Notebook."

960. O'Fallon, Kathleen. "Quest for a New Vision."

961. Morgan, Ellen. "The Golden Notebook: A Case Study in the Alienation of the Woman Writer from her own Perceptions."

962. Porter, Nancy. "Lessing's Recovery of Silenced History."

1973--Chair: Annis Pratt. Title: "The Politics of Madness in Doris Lessing's Novels."

963. Stern, Frederick C. "Doris Lessing: The Politics of Radical Humanism."

964. Pickering, Jean. "The Connection Between the 'Politics of the Left' and the 'Politics of Madness' in the Work of Doris Lessing."

965. Libby, Marion V. "Lessing and Laing: Psychopolitics and Prophecy."

966. Rubenstein, Roberta. "Briefing on Inner Space: Doris Lessing and R. D. Laing."

1974--Chair: Ellen Morgan. Title: "The Writings of Doris Lessing."

967. Carnes, Valerie. "Art as Metaphor in Doris Lessing's The Golden Notebook."

968. Christ, Carol. "Prophetic Power and Spiritual Insight in The Four-Gated City."

969. Kaplan, Sydney Janet. "Postscript: The Summer Before the Dark."

970. Solomon, Charlotte. "Mother, Must I Go on Dancing: Mothers and Daughters in Doris Lessing's Children of Violence."

971. Curkeet, Sandra. "Journal."

1975--Chair: Dee Seligman

972. Beard, Linda Susan. "Lessing's Africa."

973. Reid, Martha. "Lessing in the Classroom."

974. Gage, Diane. "The Myth of Doris Lessing."

975. Rose, Ellen Cronan. "The End of the Game: New Directions in Doris Lessing's Fiction."

976. Draine, Betsy. "The Memoirs of a Survivor: Irrationalism as the Path to Freedom."

977. Goldberg, Patsy Vigderman. "Lessing Reconsidered."

1976--Chair: Ellen Cronan Rose.

978. Draine, Betsy. "A Widening Vision: This Was the Old Chief's Country."

979. Carnes, Valerie. "Stories Within a Novel: Short Stories and Sketches in The Golden Notebook.

980. Chaffee, Patricia. "Spatial Patterns and Closed Groups in African Stories."

981. Beard, Linda Susan. "In Cyclical Time: Lessing as an African Writer."

1977—Chair: Betsy Draine. Title: "Tradition and the
Individual Talent."

982. Bazin, Nancy Topping. "Moments of Revelation in
      Sons and Lovers, Portrait of the Artist as a Young Man
      and Martha Quest."

983. Dixon, Terrell, "Doris Lessing: The Realistic
      Tradition and the New Realism."

984. Greene, Mildred Sarah. "Doris Lessing and the
      Tradition of Sensibility."

985. Peterson, Lorna. "Lessing and Dostoevsky:
      Parallels and Paradoxes."

986. Stitzel, Judith. "Language and the Rendering of
      Consciousness in Doris Lessing's Fiction: Is the
      Metaphor of the Stream Appropriate?"

987. Tiger, Virginia. "Lessing and the Tradition of the
      Confessional Novel."

1978—Chair: Lorna Peterson and Virginia Tiger. Title:
"Doris Lessing and Other Twentieth Century Visionaires."

988. LeDonne, Mary S. "The Lively Yeast: Shared Vision
      in Doris Lessing's The Four-Gated City and Aldous
      Huxley's Island."

989. McFadden-Gerber, Margaret and Leslie Gerber. "From
      Ideology to Dystopia: The Orwellian Pattern in
      Lessing's Literary Development."

990. Middleton, Victoria S. "Fiction into Fable:
      Apocalypse in The Memoirs of a Survivor."

991. Sprague, Claire. "Without Contraries There is No
      Vision: The Dispossessed and The Four-Gated City."

1979—Chair: Clair Sprague. Session cancelled by MLA;
rescheduled for 1980.

DISSERTATIONS

992. Millar, Clive John. "The Contemporary South African Short Story in English: with special reference to the work of Nadine Gordimer, Doris Lessing, Alan Paton, Jack Cope, Uys Krige, and Dan Jacobson." M. A. thesis in English, University of Cape Town (1962), 82-113.

>The first dissertation on Doris Lessing, written in East Germany.

993. Graustein, Gottfried. "Entwicklungs tendenzen im Schaffen Doris Lessings." ("Trends of Development in the Works of Doris Lessing.") Wissenschaftliche Zeitschrift der Universität Leipzig, 12 (1963), 529-533.

994. Hartwig, Dorothea. "Die Widerspiegelung Afrikanischer Probleme in Werkd Doris Lessings." ("A Reflection on the African Problem in the works of Doris Lessing.") Wissenschaftliche Zeitschrift der Universität Leipzig. 12 (1963), 87-104.

995. Carey, Father Alfred Augustine. "Doris Lessing: The Search for Reality. A Study of the Major Themes in Her Novels." DAI, 26 (1966), 3297A (University of Wisconsin).

>Five basic themes are explored: the theme of race, of communism, of generational conflict, of man-woman relationships, and of the novelist in the modern world. Carey contends that Lessing is a humanist and a philosophical novelist rather than a sociological writer. Since this thesis is the first American dissertation on Lessing, it provides an interesting starting point for the development of criticism. All of the major novels inclusive of The Golden Notebook are considered.

996. Schlueter, Paul George. "A Study of the Major Novels of Doris Lessing." DAI 29 (1969), 3619A (Southern Illinois University).

>Doris Lesisng's female protagonists desire to express their "freedom" in four areas: race, politics, sex, and reading. Their dreams "closely parallel their conscious activities and thoughts. They are thus sufficiently similar to be considered as one prototypal woman found in varying degrees in all her novels and espcially in The Golden Notebook." Only the first four novels of Children of Violence had been published at this time.

997.   Burkom, Selma Ruth. "A Reconciliation of Opposites:
       A Study of the Works of Doris Lessing." DAI, 31
       (1970), 5390A (University of Minnesota).

         An aesthetic examination of Lessing's canon.
         Her attitudes are defined as "romantic" and
         "idealistic," while her techniques are
         realistic. However, these opposites of form
         and content are synthesized when taken together.
         Lessing's vision of nature and of the romantic
         hero, modeled on Prometheus, are examined, as
         well as her eschatalogical view of the world.
         Her aesthetic is basically Coleridgean.

998.   Alcorn, Noeline Elizabeth. "Vision and Nightmare: A
       Study of Doris Lessing's Novels." DAI, 32 (1971),
       1500A (University of California, Irvine).

         "Mrs. Lessing's 'commitment' has been the
         shaping principle of all her work." However,
         she is not committed to any one ideology as much
         as to a faith in man and his future and to a
         clear description of the nightmarish present.
         The study includes all five novels of the
         Children of Violence series as well as other
         major novels.

999.   Brooks, Ellen, W. "Fragmentation and Integration: A
       Study of Doris Lessing's Fiction." DAI, 32 (1971),
       3989-3990A (New York University).

         The focus of attention of Lessing's work is
         'fragmentation, division, and disorder within
         the human personality, paralleled by conflicts
         among groups and nations." Her portrayal of
         female consciousness from the perspective of
         fragmentation is explored and her portrayal is
         compared with Charlotte Bronte and George Eliot's
         treatment of their heroines. Jung and Laing are
         also used to explore the psychological
         implications of Lessing's work.

1000. Smith, Diane E. Sherwood. "A Thematic Study of Doris
       Lessing's Children of Violence." DAI, 32 (1971),
       1530A (Loyola University of Chicago).

         Plot, character, imagery, and style of the
         Children of Violence series all have the
         'thematic intention of demonstrating the in-
         dividual's relationship to the collective.
         Lessing implies that "unless an individual can
         free himself from seeing only the partial view
         of life that any society offers to its memebers,
         he will live his life in alienation."

1001. Morgan, Delane D. "The Unity of Human Life; The Meaning of the Novels of Doris Lessing." Occidental College, 1972. (Must be ordered direct from Occidental.)

1002. Krouse, Agate Nesaule. "The Feminism of Doris Lessing." DAI, 34 (1972), 322A (University of Wisconsin).

> "The purpose of this dissertation is to determine whether Lessing's work can be described as feminist at all, to define precisely the kind of feminism evident," and to define "characteristics of literary feminism and their relationship to aesthetic value." Lessing's feminism is implicit in that she concentrates on "discrimination according to race and class rather than sex." "Lessing's control of irony, point of view, humor and specific details often allows her to utilize stereotypes successfully."

1003. Marchino, Lois Annette. "The Search for Self in the Novels of Doris Lessing." DAI, 33 (1972), 2384-2385A (University of New Mexico).

> One of the first dissertations to relate the psychological and mystical interpretations of Lessing. The need for self-knowledge, which includes the understanding of one's relationship to the collective, becomes a recognition that the self is part of a spirit of which all humanity is a part. Charles Watkins' visions "suggest the knowlege which Lessing believes must exist in all human beings."

1004. Halliday, Patricia Ann Young. "The Pursuit of Wholeness in the Work of Doris Lessing: Dualities, Mutiplicities, and the Resolution of Patterns in Illumination." DAI, 34 (1973), 2626-2627A (University of Minnesota).

> "Fragmentatons manifest themselves in thematic parallels and polarities, especially in the divisions within the self, between the self and society, between different social orders, and between men and women." Lessing uses comparison and contrast, the unconscious as a key to the conscious, conflicting time schemes, doubling of characters to get alternate views of reality." However, "all fragmentations dissolve in the cosmic perspective of illumination," which is available through many forms of altered consciousness.

1005. De Courtivron, Isabelle. "Androgyny, Misogyny, and Madness: Three Essays on Women in Literature." DAI, 32 (1974), 5905-5906A.

> The third essay of this dissertation is titled "Woman and the Visionary Experience: An Essay on Madness in Two Female Authors" and is concerned with the work of Lessing and Violette Leduc. Their exploration of inner space is compared.

1006. Naumer, Mary Ann Singleton. "The City and the Veld: A Study of the Fiction of Doris Lessing." DAI, 34 (1973), 5984-5985A (University of Oregon).

> The thesis was later published as a book with the same title. (See #256).

1007. Grant, Velma Fudge. "The Quest for Wholeness in Novels by Doris Lessing." DAI, 36 (1974), 901A (State University of New Jersey).

> "In each of her novels from Martha Quest to Briefing, Lessing consciously or unconsciously, focuses on her protagonists' attempts to achieve wholeness." Lessing is compared to Joyce, Woolf, and Lawrence in her concern for unity in divided lives.

1008. Kildahl, Karen Ann. "The Political and Apolitical Novels of Doris Lessing: A Critical Study of Children of Violence, The Golden Notebook, Briefing for a Descent into Hell." DAI, 35 (1974), 4528A (University of Washington).

> Traces Lessing's artistic and ideological development. Argues that Lessing's philosophical evolution begins with the liberal, rational assumption in social progress, based in a Marxist ethic, but moves towards a supra-rational vision of an irrational, nightmarish society which is doomed for destruction.

1009. Rose, Ellen Cronan. "Doris Lessing's Children of Violence as a Bildungsroman: An Eriksonian Analysis." DAI, 35 (1974), 3006A (University of Massachusetts, Amherst).

> The central thematic concern of all bildungsroman is the protagonist's attainment of a sense of identity, rather than simply the adolescent's coming of age. Martha, however, fails to achieve a sense of identity because her real social environment fails to confirm her own sense of identity. Only when Martha's surrogate city in the Appendix is accepted as the real world can

one establish Martha's sense of identity as a
result of a symbiosis with the world around her.
This study was later revised into a monograph,
The Tree Outside the Window (#255).

1010. Sukenick, Lynn. "Sense and Sensibility in Women's
Fiction: Studies in the Novels of George Eliot,
Virginia Woolf, Anaïs Nin, and Doris Lessing."
DAI, 35 (1974), 4563A (City University of New York).

The cultural generalization about women's
special capacity for emotions is examined from
the perspective of the listed female writers.
"For Doris Lessing, feeling is connected with
the feminine, but it is suspect, and sometimes
even perilous."

1011. King, Holly Beth. "Convenent Fictions: The Novel
Within the Novel in the Works of Doris Lessing,
André Gide, and Flann O'Brien." DAI, 36 (1975),
4470A (University of California, Los Angeles).

The Golden Notebook is the only Lessing
novel discussed, and King asserts its
significant style of a novel–within–a novel
is used for somewhat different purposes than
in the novels of Gide and O'Brien. Lessing
"portrays the struggles and pitfalls of the
'realistic' novelist whose narratives must
necessarily fall short of portraying
'reality.'" "The ultimate effect of the
technique ... is to focus on that 'reality'
above and beyond the work of which the novel
can only be a feeble imitation."

1012. Seligman, Claudia Dee. "The Autobiographical Novels
of Doris Lessing." DAI, 37 (1975), 1544A (Tufts
University).

This thesis differentiates the autobiography
from autobiographical fiction and asserts that
the latter is a useful perspective from which to
evaluate Lessing's art. "The central critical
problem in talking about Lessing's
autobiographical novels is to understand the
relationship between the author and her persona."
"Lessing's ability ... to reconcile contemporary
personal and social contradictions is directly
related to her integration with her persona in
her most autobiographical novels, Landlocked and
The Golden Notebook." The latter novel is
explored as a pivotal work of this style and one
in which a new form of consciousness emerges.
"The self which is created is more integrated: it
is both personal and social, both individual and
collective, both female and male, both the

product of historically 'true facts' and
'imaginatively true fictions.'" This thesis
also includes original biographical material in
the form of four interviews made with Lessing's
friends and relatives in Rhodesia in 1973
(published by Modern Fiction Studies, Spring
1980).

1013. McLaughlin, Marilou Briggs. "The Love Dialectic."
DAI, 36 (1976), 8035A (State University of New York
at Binghamton).

This thesis is a comparative study of The Golden
Notebook with Katherine Anne Porter's Ship of
Fools, Joyce Carol Oates' Them, and Christina
Stead's The Man Who Loved Children. The
dialectic of romantic love as both human fulfillment and as a deception which disguises
misogyny is examined. The author wishes to see
if these women writers have "slanted the argu-
ments," and concludes that none of the novels
"charge men with total responsibility for the
failure of love." Each novelist suggests that it
is women's dependence on romantic love for self-
fulfillment which is the mistake.

1014. Wells, Dorothy Berquist. "The Unity of Doris
Lessing's Children of Violence." DAI, 37
(1976), 1573-1574A (Tulane University).

The purpose of this dissertation is to argue
that Children of Violence has a basic unifying
design in spite of the obvious changes which
occurred both in its intellectual content and
in its form." Lessing's stated theme--the
relationship of the individual to the collective
conscience--remains the same, although after
The Golden Notebook she becomes skeptical of
received knowledge and logic while becoming
more convinced of non-rational forms of
understanding.

1015. Johnson, Sally H. "Form and Philosophy in the Novels
of Doris Lessing." DAI, 38 (1976), 282A (University
of Connecticut).

Discussion of the inherent tensions in Lessing's
philosophical beliefs between "an affirmative
vision and the destructive forces which limit
man's potential." Lessing's ambivalence about
the nature of man and his capacity for change
translates to "thematic deflations, problematic
characterizations, abrupt changes in tone,
ambiguous endings, and symbolic resolutions."
Johnson suggests that both Sufism and Marxism
held essentially religious meaning to Lessing,

and that her loss of faith in language is
directly related to her disillusionment with
socialism and her interest in mysticism. There
is a tension in Lessing's work between politics,
which does not change, and private consciousness,
which does change. "The theorectical assertion
of human goodness is inevitably undercut."

1016. Martens, Lorna. "The Diary Novel and Contemporary
Fiction: Studies in Max Frisch, Michel Butor, and
Doris Lessing." DAI, 38 (1976), 247A (Yale
University).

"This dissertation is a study of the diary as
a narrative structure in contemporary fiction
and its historical backgrounds in England,
France, and Germany." All three of these
writers "retain the single point of view and
day-to-day temporality...[but they] exploit the
diary's potential for discontinuity and open-
endedness." Each writer uses the diary to
express an oblique message, and form itself
becomes a means of expression, since all three
writers demonstrate a distrust of language in
these works. In The Golden Notebook, "wholeness" is "reduced and distorted by any given
mode of verbal representation."

1017. Draine, Mary Elizabeth. "Stages of Consciousness
in Doris Lessing's Fiction." DAI, 38 (1977),
2138A (Temple University).

Lessing has, from her earliest stories, been
working out the relationship between her sense
of determinism and her faith in the human
consciousness and its ability to liberate the
individual by recognizing the social and
psychological boundaries. This Was the Old
Chief's Country, The Grass is Singing,
Children of Violence, The Golden Notebook, and
Memoirs are all considered in this conflict
between freedom and fatalism. Draine posits
that there is a unity of vision in the
Children of Violence series which is absent in
Memoirs of a Survivor.

1018. McKeon, Nancy T. "Conscious Construction: The
Concept of Plot in Five Novels by Women." DAI,
38 (1977), 2115A (Loyola University of Chicago).

"This study attempts to establish that, from
the outset, women have been conscious of the
technical requirements of their craft, and in
fact,have used plot as a major tool through
which to express artistic maturity and
innovation." Lessing's work in The Golden

Notebook reveals that plot itself can be used
"as a tool for the exploration of the chaos
of contemporary society."

1019. Cederstrom, Lorelei. "From Marxism to Myth: A
Developmental Study of the Novels of Doris Lessing."
DAI, 38 (1978), 7320A (University of Manitoba,
Canada). Order direct from University.

Lessing has moved, in the novels since The Golden
Notebook (1962), away from Marxism to a Jungian
emphasis on self-analysis and "inward exploration." Convinced that society can change only
when the individual changes, Lessing attempts
to move the reader "beyond ordinary patterns of
perceptions." Through the "formal experimentation of The Golden Notebook and Briefing" and
through "documentation of the psychological
journey in The Four-Gated City and Memoirs,
"Lessing enters us into the psyche. The way
out is "through archetypal patterns and cosmic
analogies."

1020. Gage, Diane Burdick. "Fictive Figurings: Metacommentary on Doris Lessing's Children of Violence."
DAI, 39 (1978), 896A (Arizona State University).

Children of Violence is considered as a "metafiction," that is fiction which is about fiction.
It requires "metacommentary," in which the
reader's relation to the text is important.
When subjects and objects merge in Landlocked,
Gage asserts that it becomes necessary to use
this type of reading and particularly to use it
for The Four-Gated City, in which Martha
functions not only as character but also as
reader-in-the-text.

1021. Mitchell, Tamara K. "The Irrational Elements in
Doris Lessing's Fiction." DAI, 38 (1978), 7326A
(Boston University).

"The purpose of this work has been to discover
how Lessing represented...irrational elements...
how that experience works within the whole
fictional work, and how Lessing's vision of the
irrational has developed and changed." Lessing
moves from writing naturalistic tragedy to
heroic fiction to novels of irrationalism which
document the expanded consciousness concommitant
with the experience of the irrational.

1022. Walter, Donna Joanne. "Twentieth-Century Woman in
       the Early Novels of Doris Lessing." DAI, 39 (1978),
       3608A (The University of Tennessee).

       This thesis is a "study of the major influences
       affecting Lessing's characterization of female
       protagonists, both adolescent and adult, in the
       novels from The Grass is Singing through
       Landlocked." The woman character which Lessing
       creates seeks wholeness and faces chaos, is
       sexual and feminine,but "not driven by her
       sexuality;" "she is intelligent enough to over-
       come ambivalence;" "she is political though
       powerless; "she is responsible to the human
       collective though often in despair."

1023. Wichmann, Brigitte. "From Sex-Role Identification
       Toward Androgyny: A Study of the Major Works of
       Simone de Beauvoir, Doris Lessing, and Christa
       Wolf." DAI, 39 (1978), 2934A.

       Each of the three women writers of this thesis
       "make an important contribution to the defini-
       tion of women." De Beauvoir's work marks the
       first stage of analysis of sex roles; Lessing's
       work suggests the second stage of conflicting
       self-acceptance and self-denial as the woman
       struggles to move beyond cultural roles.
       Wolf's work represents the third phase in
       which sex roles are absent and individuals move
       toward androgyny.

1024. Hightower, Sallie Turner. "Moral and Ego Develop-
       ment Stages in the Characters of Doris Lessing,
       Margaret Drabble, and John Fowles: An Analytical
       Evaluation Based on the Theories of Erik Erikson,
       Jane Loevinger and Lawrence Kohlberg." (1979),
       (University of Houston).

       Erikson's ideas are used in connection with
       "Jack Orkney" and The Summer Before the Dark.

BIBLIOGRAPHY ON LESSING

1025. Burkom, Selma R. "A Doris Lessing Checklist."
       Critique, 11 (1969), 51-68.

1026. Burkom, Selma R. and Margaret Williams. Doris
       Lessing: A Checklist of Primary and Secondary
       Sources. Troy, New York: The Whitston Publishing
       Co., 1973.

       The most complete bibliography prior to
       this one.

1027. Anonymous. "Doris Lessing." In Contemporary Authors. Detroit: Gale Research, 1974, 509-513.

An encyclopedic entry on Lessing which gives an overview of her work and long excerpts from book reviews.

1028. Ipp, Catharina. Doris Lessing: A Bibliography. Johannesburg: University of Witswatersand, 1967.

1029. Krouse, Agate Nesaule. "A Doris Lessing Checklist." Contemporary Literature, 14 (Autumn 1973), 590-597.

1030. Lessing, Doris. unpublished typescripts of The Memoirs of a Survivor and The Temptation of Jack Orkney. Special Collections of the McFarlin Library, University of Tulsa, Tulsa, Oklahoma.

1031. Marchino, Lois. "Papers on Doris Lessing: An Introductory Comment." World Literature Written in English, 12 (November 1973), 148-150.

An overview of a collection of four essays on Lessing in this issue.

1032. Myers, Carol Fairbanks. Women in Literature: Criticism of the Seventies. Metuchen, New Jersey: The Scarecrow Press, 1976, 117-121.

1033. Pichanik, J., A. J. Chennells and L. B. Rix. Rhodesian Literature in English: A Bibliography. (1890-1974/5). (Gwelo, Rhodesia: Mambo Press, 1977). Mambo Press, Senga Road, POBox 779, Gwelo, Zimbabwe.

An important bibliography which lists short stories and poems published in Africa between 1943-49. This information was available too late to be included in the current work but should be of great interest for many.

1034. Roberts, R. S. "A Select Bibliography on Doris Lessing." Zambesia: The Journal of the University of Rhodesia, 4 (December 1976), 99-101.

1035. Seligman, Dee. "Checklist of Doris Lessing Criticism." Doris Lessing Newsletter, 2 (Summer, 1978), 5, 12.

Criticism of Lessing during 1977 is documented.

1036. Seligman, Dee. "Dissertations on Doris Lessing." Doris Lessing Newsletter, 2 (Summer 1978), 7.

1037. Seligman, Dee. "Lessing on Tape." Doris Lessing Newsletter, 3 (Winter 1979), 5.

1038. Seligman, Dee. "Lessing Short Story Bibliography."
      Doris Lessing Newsletter, 2 (Summer 1978), 5.

1039. Seligman, Dee. "Published Interviews with Lessing."
      Doris Lessing Newsletter, 3 (Winter 1979) 5.

RESEARCH/TEACHING SUGGESTIONS

1040. Betts, Jane Colville. "Doris Lessing: A College
      Course." University of Wisconsin-Extension,
      Department of Liberal Studies, 1978.

> A course handbook which is useful both for
> those reading Lessing for the first time and
> for those teaching her works. The booklet is
> divided into: a general introduction on
> Lessing's biography, literary reputation, and
> comments on her style; a chapter on the
> adolescent novel, using Martha Quest as its
> focus, two chapters on The Golden Notebook,
> including a segment on the form of the novel,
> and two chapters on the mystical novels and
> the novel of madness, using Briefing as an
> example. A bibliography and suggested paper
> topics is also included.

1041. Pratt, Annis. "Introduction." Contemporary
      Literature, 14 (Autumn 1973), 413-418.

> This article basically introducess a group
> of essays on Lessing; however, Pratt gives
> suggestions for archetypal criticism on
> Lessing.

1042. Schlueter, Paul. "A Sample Course on Lessing."
      Doris Lessing Newsletter, 2 (Summer 1978), 3, 11.

> A list of suggested paper topics on
> Lessing drawn from Schlueter's course on
> her at the New School for Social Research,
> New York City. This list is particularly
> useful for teachers.

1043. Schlueter, Paul. "Schlueter on Lessing Scholar-
      ship." Doris Lessing Newsletter, 2 (Summer 1978),
      6, 12.

> Suggests areas of criticism on Lessing which
> should be addressed.

1044. Sullivan, Victoria. "Some Notes on Loss of
      Innocence: Teaching Lessing's A Man and Two Women

in an Urban Catholic College." Doris Lessing
Newsletter, 3 (Summer 1979), 12.

Provides a practical guide to the pitfalls
of teaching this short story collection.

1045. Whitlock, Gillian. "What Still Needs to Be 'Done'
on Lessing?" Doris Lessing Newsletter, 3 (Summer
1979), 8, 11.

"Not enough work has been done on the
traditionalism of Lessing's characters, the
literary conventions that they relate to, or
the style of her fiction and the conservatism
of Lessing's ideas about literature and
literary criticism." Lessing's work is a good
place for the feminist critic to "reassess the
principles of this form of literary criticism..."

INDEX TO TITLES

988, 991, 998, 999, 1000,1003,1004,1005, 1007,
1008, 1009, 1012, 1014, 1015, 1017, 1019, 1020,
1021.

Fourteen Poems

68, 69, 70, 71, 72, 73, 74, 1033.

Going Home

77, 229, 247, 257, 622, 624, 625, 663.

The Golden Notebook

6, 36, 90, 150, 152, 161, 167, 173, 186, 208, 237,
239, 242, 247, 248, 250, 251, 253, 254, 256, 257,
258, 260, 261, 262, 263, 265, 268, 269, 272, 274,
276, 277, 278, 279, 281, 282, 283, 284, 286, 287,
289, 291, 292, 293, 294, 296, 297, 298, 299, 301,
302, 306, 308, 309, 310, 311, 312, 314, 316, 322,
324. 328, 329, 330, 335, 338, 339, 342, 347, 356,
359, 363, 366, 368, 369, 370, 374, 376, 378, 379,
386, 387, 388, 390, 391, 392, 394, 395, 397, 578,
579, 580, 581, 582, 583, 584, 585, 586, 587, 588,
589, 590, 591, 592, 593, 594, 595, 596, 597, 598,
599, 600, 601, 602, 603, 604, 605, 606, 607, 608,
609, 610, 611, 612, 613, 614, 615, 616, 617, 618,
619, 620, 621, 955, 956, 957, 959, 961, 963, 964,
967, 979, 983, 984, 986, 987, 989, 995, 996, 997,
998, 999, 1001, 1002, 1003, 1004, 1006, 1007, 1008,
1010, 1011, 1012, 1013, 1016, 1017, 1018, 1019,
1021, 1022, 1040.

The Grass is Singing

1, 137, 139, 144, 145, 146, 148, 157, 163, 170,
177, 180, 184, 190, 202, 206, 247, 248, 251, 254,
256, 257, 258, 295, 322, 346, 354, 372, 393, 626,
627, 628, 629, 630, 631, 632, 633, 634, 635, 636,
637, 638, 639, 640, 641, 642, 643, 644, 645, 646,
992, 993, 1017, 1022.

The Habit of Loving

14, 30, 49, 50, 51, 62, 141, 200, 210, 305, 357,
358, 647, 648, 649, 650, 651, 652, 653, 654, 655,
656, 657, 658, 659, 660, 661, 662, 663, 664, 665,
666.

In Pursuit of the English

48, 79, 247, 667, 668, 669, 670, 671, 672, 673,
674, 675, 676, 677, 678, 679, 680, 681, 682, 683,
684, 685, 686, 687, 688, 689, 690, 691, 692, 693,
694.

Landlocked

7, 221, 247, 248, 251, 252, 255, 256, 257, 266,
280, 298, 300, 362, 506, 507, 508, 509, 510, 511,
512, 513, 514, 515, 516, 517, 518, 519, 520, 521,
522, 523.

A Man and Two Women

15, 25, 27, 34, 35, 37, 38, 39, 40, 57, 60, 143,
150, 181, 182, 189, 201, 209, 215, 247, 262, 264,
305, 318, 353, 357, 358, 695, 696, 697, 698, 699,
700, 701, 702, 703, 704, 705, 706, 707, 708, 709,
710, 712, 713, 714, 715, 716, 717, 1044.

Martha Quest

2, 158, 196, 203, 207, 216, 247, 248, 250, 251,
252, 254, 255, 256, 257, 258, 261, 262, 263, 266,
277, 279, 280, 294, 298, 303, 321, 322, 325, 336,
344, 350, 351, 355, 362, 366, 368, 369, 370, 382,
383, 387, 388, 476, 477, 478, 479, 480, 481, 482,
483, 484, 485, 486, 487, 488, 489, 490, 491, 492,
493, 494, 495, 496, 497, 498, 499, 500, 501, 502,
503, 504, 955, 956, 957, 958, 960, 962, 970, 982,
983, 993, 995, 996, 997, 998, 999, 1000, 1002,
1003, 1004, 1006, 1007, 1008, 1009, 1012, 1014,
1015, 1017, 1020, 1022, 1023, 1040.

The Memoirs of a Survivor

11, 151, 156, 187, 222, 256, 258, 290, 335, 338,
340, 341, 355, 360, 364, 398, 718, 719, 720, 721,
722, 723, 724, 725, 726, 727, 728, 729, 730, 731,
732, 733, 734, 735, 736, 737, 738, 739, 740, 741,
742, 743, 744, 745, 746, 747, 748, 749, 750, 751,
752, 753, 754, 755, 756, 757, 758, 759, 760, 761,
975, 976, 986, 989, 990, 1017, 1019, 1021, 1030.

Mr. Dolinger

64, 357, 764, 765.

Particularly Cats

41, 81, 211, 766, 767, 768, 769, 770, 771, 772,
773, 774, 775, 776, 777.

Play with a Tiger

57, 142, 174, 289, 332, 357, 778, 779, 780, 781,
1012.

A Proper Marriage

3, 171, 175, 218, 247, 248, 250, 252, 254, 255,
256, 257, 258, 261, 262, 266, 277, 279, 280, 284,

This Was the Old Chief's Country

12, 16, 18, 19, 21, 22, 23, 45, 47, 53, 55, 56,
140, 165, 179, 194, 197, 198, 199, 212, 247, 251,
256, 257, 262, 305, 323, 934, 935, 936, 937, 938,
939, 940, 941, 942, 943, 944, 945, 946, 947, 948,
949, 954, 972, 978, 981, 1006, 1017.

The Truth About Billy Newton

66, 367, 375, 950, 951, 952, 953.

Winter in July

12, 16, 18, 21, 23, 45, 47, 55, 56, 140, 165, 179,
194, 197, 198, 199, 212, 247, 251, 256, 257, 262,
934, 935, 936, 937, 938, 939, 940, 941, 942, 943,
944, 945, 946, 947, 948, 949, 954, 972, 978, 981,
1006, 1017.

INDEX TO PROPER NAMES

About the Compiler

DEE SELIGMAN received her Ph.D. in English from Tufts University in Medford, Massachusetts, and has taught there, at Bentley College in Waltham, Massachusetts, and at Boston University. She is founder and past editor of the *Doris Lessing Newsletter*, and Executive Secretary of the Doris Lessing Society, an MLA Allied Organization.